New Kittredge Shakespeare

William Shakespeare

PERICLES

PRINCE OF TYRE

William Shakespeare

PERICLES

PRINCE OF TYRE

Editor
Jeffrey Kahan
University of La Verne

Series Editor
James H. Lake
Louisiana State University,
Shreveport

Edited by George Lyman Kittredge.
Used with permission from the heirs to the Kittredge estate.
New material by Jeffrey Kahan used with permission.

Cover Design by Guy Wetherbee | Elk Amino Design, New England | elkaminodesign.com

Cover: Surf on a Rocky Coast, 1835 (oil on canvas), Achenbach, Andreas (1815–1910) / Hamburger Kunsthalle, Hamburg, Germany / The Bridgeman Art Library International.

ISBN: 978-1-58510-313-3
ISBN 10: 1-58510-313-6

Printed in the United States of America

10 9 8 7 6 5 4 3 2 1

0909TS

TABLE OF CONTENTS

Publisher's Note

George Lyman Kittredge was one of the foremost American Shakespeare scholars of the 20th century. The New Kittredge Shakespeare, builds on his celebrated scholarship and extensive notes. Each edition contains a new, updated introduction, with comments on contemporary film versions of the play, new and revised notes, including performance notes, an essay on reading the play as performance, plus topics for discussion and an annotated bibliography and filmography. For this an accomplished Shakespeare and film scholar has been commissioned to modernize each volume.

The series focuses on understanding the language and allusions in the play as well as encountering Shakespeare as performance. The audience ranges from students at all levels, as well as to readers interested in encountering the text in the context of performance on stage or film.

Ron Pullins, Publisher
Newburyport, 2009

Acknowledgments

I am grateful to the University of La Verne for a sabbatical to complete this edition. I owe as great a debt of thanks to James H. Lake, Series Editor of the New Kittredge Shakespeare, for the opportunity to work on *Pericles*. The time I have spent on this project has only strengthened my attachment to this remarkable and magical play. I would be remiss if I were not to mention Kate Welch of the Shakespeare Institute and Helen Hargest of The Shakespeare Centre Library and Archive for their collective assistance in charting *Pericles'* erratic stage journeys. Lastly, this edition was strengthened by the kind, helpful, and insightful comments of David Werner, Linda Diering, and Hannah Chapelle Wojciehowski.

Jeffrey Kahan

INTRODUCTION

Pericles: A Dark Biblical Story with Pagan Enchantments

Pericles begins with John Gower coming on stage. Gower is not a character of Shakespeare's creation but is, in fact, an actual and—even in Shakespeare's time— long-dead author. Rising from the grave, Gower tells us a story, but not one of his own devising. Rather, this author tells us a story that comes from the pen of yet another, presumably even older author.[1] It's tempting to see Gower as a stand-in for Shakespeare here, both authors retelling stories that came down from a golden age; stories that are oft repeated at "festivals,/On ember-eves and holy-ales" (1.0.5-6).

And what a story it is! The first time we meet Prince Pericles, he is about to risk his life to win the hand of a fair princess. The charming context, however, soon turns grim: there are crimes of incest in Antiochus' court which Pericles uncovers and from which he must flee. His escape from one peril leads to still other adventures: Pericles is shipwrecked on foreign shores; he soon makes his way to the court of the good King Simonides, where he wins the love of yet another princess, this one as faithful as the other was falsehearted. Pericles and his bride, Thaisa, now great with child, happily set sail to the prince's kingdom of Tyre. But a sinister storm brews, the skies thunder and flash, the billows roll, surge, and snap, and Thaisa, in the wet misery of the storm, dies while giving birth to a daughter. The grieving prince seals his wife in a casket filled with jewels and casts her into the furious sea. In the morning, her coffin is found by some villagers, who take it to Cerimon, a local healer and wizard, who uses science, music, and magic to revive the seemingly-dead princess. Suddenly inspired with religious fervor, Thaisa decides to dedicate her remaining years to the worship of the goddess Diana. Meanwhile, Pericles leaves his infant daughter Marina with King Cleon and Queen Dionyza of Tarsus. The years pass, and Marina, now a beautiful woman, is much beloved by everyone in Tarsus—everyone that is, except Queen Dionyza, who believes that

---

1   A number of editions to the play are cited in this Introduction. Their full bibliographical references can be found in the Bibliography and Filmography (pg. 101). Shakespeare's Gower probably has in mind Godfrey of Viterbo's *Pantheon* (ca.1186). See Alfred R. Bellinger, Yale Shakespeare ed. 1925: 112-14.

her own daughter is overshadowed by Marina's gracious beauty. Dionyza soon hires Leonine to kill the princess. Amazingly, Marina escapes only to be kidnapped by pirates. Nonetheless, Leonine informs Dionyza that Marina is dead. She and King Cleon agree to tell Pericles that Marina died suddenly and of natural causes. Upon hearing that his daughter is dead, Pericles falls into a deep and burying depression. He might have been still more disconsolate were he to have learned that Marina survived an attempted assassination only to be sold to a brothel in the port city of Mytilene, where men bid to be the first to rape her. As horrible as this sounds, the situation soon turns comic when all her libidinous customers are chastened by her purity and modesty, including Lysimachus, governor of the town. Marina leaves the brothel, her virginity still intact, and teaches the women of the town to sing, weave, sew, and dance. When Pericles' ship arrives at Mytilene, Lysimachus wonders if Marina's loveliness might not cheer the grief-stricken prince. She plays her harp and sings, but Pericles remains bleak and impassive, until Marina tells him the story of her life. When Pericles realizes that his daughter lives, he is overjoyed and, moments later, hearing the miraculous music of the gods, falls into a trace in which Diana, the goddess of chastity, orders him to make sacrifice at her temple in Ephesus. Pericles obeys the divine decree and is there reunited with his long-lost wife Thaisa. The good news continues. Lysimachus, who helped save Marina from the brothel in Mytilene, asks Pericles for Marina's hand in honorable marriage. The play closes with Gower assuring us that Antiochus, Dionyza, and all other evil-doers are punished for their crimes.

As Algernon Charles Swinburne has noted, Pericles is not someone we are likely to meet, except in the classical writings of Homer or in the Testaments of the Hebrews and Christians.[2] Certainly, Thaisa's and Marina's respective returns from the dead suggest a Shakespearean interest in resurrection myths. Likewise, Marina's miraculous ability to shield herself from danger may suggest the broad outlines of Daniel in the lion's den. To most, however, Pericles' suffering recalls the biblical story of Job: a stormy life, unendurable, undeserved, and seemingly unceasing. Setting aside biblical parallels for the moment, we may certainly agree that Pericles' labors rival those of Greek myth. The incest of Antiochus' court mirrors that of Oedipus; his shipwreck recalls the misadventures of Odysseus, the pawn of Circe's lust and Hera's vengeance; Cerimon's revival of Thaisa echoes Orpheus' music-charming attempt to save Eurydice. These mythic devices may seem farfetched in our world, dominated by politics, paperwork, student loans, and mortgage payments. Shakespeare's evocation of this long-dead poet, who evokes a still older poet, may only further increase that seemingly unbridgeable distance. That was then; this is now. The time of heroes, if it ever existed, is no longer.

And yet we should not dismiss fiction because it violates our rational considerations. Pericles is not a journey through history or geography; it is not a

---

2   Algernon Charles Swinburne, *Pericles and Other Studies* (London: For Private Circulation, 1914), 17.

record of battles, of zero-sum gains and net losses. Those factual narratives, valuable in their own right, can be measured as true or false against historical records. *Pericles* is a story of poetry and the imagination, one in which we journey back in time to walk with and, in a deeper sense, *as* the prince, losing ourselves as he lost himself and finding, as he found, something profound in the experience.

Profundity, however, is not the same as power. In video games, the hero, after the defeat of each enemy, often collects more abilities and, hence, more control over his world, but in *Pericles* the prince is weakened after each contest. He came to Antioch with a free and open heart. He no sooner saw a king but thought him noble; he no sooner saw a princess but loved her entirely. His willingness to gamble life for love was a sign of his own confidence. Death, Pericles, believed, was no match for him. After the revelation of incest and the threat of assassination, that self-assurance is taken from him, so much so that when he comes to Pentapolis, Pericles worries that the much-respected King Simonides is, like Antiochus, a tyrant and a murderer:

> 'Tis the King's subtlety to have my life.—
> O, seek not to entrap me, gracious lord,
> A stranger and distressed gentleman,
> That never aim'd so high to love your daughter,
> But bent all offices to honor her.   (2.5.42–46)

The once-valiant prince is now all too willing to set aside his love of a princess to save his own skin. Although Pericles is mistaken about Simonides—who is joyful that his daughter has found so good a man—the prince's luck is short lived. Upon the (presumed) deaths of his wife and daughter, Pericles' spirit is broken still further. He is alone and wishes only to be left alone; a "grieving Howard Hughes, with uncut hair and unending silences."[3] Thaisa, too, retreats from human contact. After her miraculous revival, she longs for nothing more than the life of a sequestered nun. As for Marina, her suffering seems to be yet another variation of her father's longing for physical and emotional isolation. Marina's refusal to be physically exploited is understandable and laudable. Her refusal to discuss her royal parentage with the tangibly noble Lysimachus, on the other hand, suggests a voluntary and unnecessary emotional isolation analogous to her father's self-imposed seclusion.

In the "How to Read *Pericles, Prince of Tyre* as Performance" section of this edition, I argue that these various inward turnings are thematically linked to Antiochus' act of incest. The argument is not without controversy and may well agitate some readers. What we can say firmly and less controversially is that what draws Pericles out of his dejection is not his faith, for he questions the wisdom of the gods at 3.1.22-24, nor his love of Marina, for the woman he meets in 5.1 is a stranger to him, but his compassion for others. Pericles is a prince exiled from his own kingdom and mired in his own losses. Hearing the tragic tale of a Mytilene

3   Benedict Nightingale, "Pericles: the comeback." *The Times*, September 20, 2003. The same comparison is made by Michael Billington, though in reference to Rob Edwards' Pericles (Dir. David Thacker, RSC, 1990). See his article, "Pericles reborn." *The Guardian*, April 14, 1990.

slave girl, the prince pities and, in that act, is liberated from anguish. Strangers are suddenly kindred spirits. In our identification with Pericles, or, variously, with Thaisa and Marina, we, as readers and audience members, are taken, however transiently, out of ourselves. In feeling their pain, we are freed from our own; in seeing them rise out of the depths of despair, we are similarly unchained from the narrow, inward interests of our daily existence.

Source Materials

Scholars have long identified John Gower's *Confessio Amantis* (composed ca.1386; published 1390) as Shakespeare's primary source. There are occasional echoes of Gower's phrases throughout the play. The most striking is at 3.2.107, where Shakespeare preserved Gower's very words: "Where am I?/ Where is my lorde, what worlde is this?"[4] But Shakespeare also departed from his sources in many notable instances: in Gower's version, Antiochus' daughter is raped; in Shakespeare's *Pericles*, she is a willing victim; in Gower, Pericles is employed by Simonides as a music teacher for his daughter; in Shakespeare's version, he is not. Further, Simonides' wife is alive in Gower and plays an active role in matching her daughter with the prince; in Shakespeare's version, she is never mentioned.

Shakespeare was also indebted to Laurence Twine's *The Patterne of Painefull Adventures*, registered in 1576 and reprinted as late as 1607. Here too, Shakespeare rejected important details: in Twine, Marina, newly sold into sexual slavery, is made to bow before a golden statue of the god Priapus. No such scene exists in *Pericles*. Further notable differences: In *Patterne of Painefull Adventures*, Lysimachus, renamed Athanagoras, has a daughter, presumably from a prior marriage; in *Pericles*, he does not. Finally, Twine's *Patterne of Painefull Adventures* extends the story to long after the curtain fall of events in *Pericles*; these final details include the birth of Pericles' son, Altistrates.

Philip Sidney's *Arcadia* (composed ca.1570s-80s; published 1590) has also been proposed as a minor source. As Kittredge noted, the name "Pericles" may or may not be a perversion of the name of "Pyrocles," a much-shipwrecked hero in Sidney's *Arcadia*.[5] If the link is justified, the play may be read didactically, at least according to Mary Judith Dunbar, who noted that Pyrocles' various misfortunes are a romantic presentment of ethical and political themes essential to "the education of princes."[6] The Arden editor F.D. Hoeniger further suggests that Sidney's *Arcadia* "exercised considerable influence on the play's language."[7]

---

4   Geoffrey Bullough, *Narrative and Dramatic Sources of Shakespeare*. 8 vols. (London, Routledge and Kegan Paul; New York, Columbia University Press, 1957-75),Vol. VI: 401. The line corresponds to Gower's *Confessio Amantis*, BK VIII, line 1214-1215.

5   Kittredge ed. 1936: 1378.

6   Mary Judith Dunbar, *Pericles: A Study of Dramatic Construction* (Ph.D Dissertation, Stanford University, 1976), 42.

7   Hoeniger, Arden ed. 1963: XIX.

The Possible Role of George Wilkins

Pericles has a loose, episodic structure that has puzzled critics, many of whom have also complained that the play feels somehow less dense than other Shakespeare plays written around the same time: *King Lear, Antony and Cleopatra*, and *Coriolanus*. Defining Shakespearean destiny is difficult, if not impossible, but there are a number of contradictions and discrepancies in the text itself which suggest that the structure of the play has been damaged. At 2.5.24-27, Simonides compliments Pericles on his performance of a song, a worthy dramatic moment, but one that is not in the extant play. Another song is missing in 5.1.76.*sd*.[8] At 5.3.77-78, we learn that Thaisa has been receiving mail that keeps her abreast of events in her father's kingdom. If so, why did she never think to write him with news of her miraculous revival? Many scholars have argued that the disjointed and illogical plot is the result of a failed collaboration: Acts 1-2 were penned by George Wilkins, who in 1608 also wrote the prose narrative *The Painfull Adventures of Pericles Prince of Tyre, Being the True History of the Play of Pericles, as it was lately presented by the worthy and ancient poet John Gower*.[9] According to this theory, Shakespeare was brought in to write Acts 3-5 but never fully integrated his contribution with the earlier scenes.

Let us first deal with Wilkins, who seems to have been a thoroughly unlikeable man: Records indicate that he had brushes with the law several times, including an arrest in 1610 for being a pimp and for "kicking a woman on the belly which was then great with childe."[10] Given Wilkins' shady background, some critics have suggested that he, not Shakespeare, wrote the brothel scenes (4.2 and 4.6).[11] Assigning one set of lines, passages or scenes to Shakespeare and another set to Wilkins is not without its problems. In the early to mid twentieth century, George Brandes, Walter Raleigh, Kenneth Deighton and George Lyman Kittridge noted that *Measure for Measure* features a variety of brothel scenes, and, therefore, Shakespeare was quite capable of writing 4.2 and 4.6 himself; in a more recent study, Marjorie Garber

---

8   Hoeniger discusses this and other missing songs in his edition (Arden ed. 1963: LXXVIII).

9   F.D. Hoeniger has argued that Wilkins and another playwright, John Day, "with perhaps yet a third dramatist," wrote the first two acts, and Shakespeare, who had become "sufficiently interested in their venture," wrote the rest. He later recanted the possibility that Shakespeare would stoop to collaborating with "a hackwriter like George Wilkins." See his Arden ed. 1963: LXIII; see also 171-80; F.D. Hoeniger, "Gower and Shakespeare in *Pericles*." *Shakespeare Quarterly* 33(1982): 461-79; 463. Brian Vickers, argues that Wilkins wrote Acts 1-2. See his *Shakespeare Co-Author* (Oxford: Oxford University Press, 2002), 291-332.

10   Charles Nicholl, *The Lodger Shakespeare* (New York and London: Viking/Penguin, 2007), 201.

11   See MacDonald P. Jackson concludes that they are "largely," though not completely, by Shakespeare. *Defining Shakespeare: 'Pericles' as Test Case* (Oxford: Oxford University Press, 2003): 232. At the turn of the Twentieth Century, other critics argued that Rowley, Dekker, Heywood or Chapman had a hand in writing the brothel scenes. For an overview, see Alfred R. Bellinger, *Yale Shakespeare* ed. 1925: 126-27.

has concluded that the "brothel scenes are surely by Shakespeare."[12] On the other hand, as the Oxford editor Roger Warren hypothesizes, if Shakespeare collaborated with Wilkins he also very probably rewrote Wilkins and Wilkins probably rewrote Shakespeare, thus rendering futile any attempt to locate a purely Wilkinsian or Shakespearean passage.[13] Lastly, New Cambridge editors Doreen DelVecchio and Anthony Hammond argue that many of the supposedly purely Shakespearean scenes in *Pericles* (Acts 3-5) are, on occasion, just as "contorted" and "tortuous" as anything written in the earlier Acts supposedly composed by George Wilkins. The theory that Shakespeare was, on occasion, as bad a writer as Wilkins does not prove that Wilkins was not involved, nor does it prove that he was. Thus, they cautiously argue that Shakespeare wrote the entire play himself.[14]

Printhouse Issues and Editorial Interventions

Further complicating our ability to discover who, if anyone, aided Shakespeare in the writing of *Pericles* is the inferiority of the early printed copy. Virtually all scholars agree that the play as originally published has some passages that are virtually unintelligible, but there is ongoing disagreement as to why this is so.[15] It is possible that the fault lies with the original printer, Henry Gosson, who

---

12   George Brandes, *William Shakespeare: A Critical Study*. 2 vols. (London: Heinemann, 1898), II:290; Walter Raleigh, *Shakespeare* (London: Macmillan and Co., 1907), 53; Kenneth Deighton, Arden ed., 1907: XIX; Kittredge ed. 1936: 1377; Marjorie Garber, *Shakespeare After All* (New York: Anchor Books/Random House, 2004), 758.

13   Roger Warren, Oxford ed. 2003: 69. Warren was in part anticipated by William Hazlitt, who speculated that many of the most Shakespearean bits in *Pericles* may have been the work of a clever imitator. See William Hazlitt, *Lectures on the Literature of the Age of Elizabeth, and Characters of Shakespear's Plays* (London: George Bell and Sons, 1890), 243. S.T. Coleridge argued that Shakespeare rewrote an older play and only "troubled himself to put in a thought or image" in the early parts but then grew interested as he progressed onwards. Consequently, the "the last two acts are almost altogether by him." See Samuel Taylor Coleridge, *Shakespearean Criticism*. Ed. Thomas Middleton Raysor. 2 vols. 2nd ed. London: J.M. Dent and Sons; New York: E.P. Dutton and Co., Inc., 1960, II:165. Likewise, Kenneth Muir argued that the version we now have was so heavily revised by Shakespeare as to retain only occasional words or phrases of the original play, which may have been written by George Wilkins or some other playwright, possibly Thomas Heywood. See his edition *The Painfull Adventures of Pericles, Prince of Tyre* (Liverpool: University of Liverpool, 1953), X-XII. See also Jackson, who argues that Shakespeare's prose is more Wilkinsian than his verse (*Defining Shakespeare: 'Pericles' as Test Case*, 206).

14   Doreen DelVecchio and Anthony Hammond, New Cambridge Shakespeare ed. 1985, 11-13. See also G. Wilson Knight, who argues that the play has a remarkable "internal coherence" and cites numerous instances, even in the first two acts, of lines and situations corresponding to Shakespeare's earlier works (*The Crown of Life*. London, New York, Toronto: Geoffrey Cumberledge/ Oxford University Press, 1947. 39-44 and 75). See also Philip Edwards, who described Wilkins as a "fifth rate writer" and raised the possibility that Shakespeare wrote the entire play himself (New Penguin ed. 1976; rev.1996: 196 and 39).

15   Brian Vickers, 297.

seems to have been particularly slovenly in setting the manuscript.[16] Alternatively, Stephen Orgel argues that Gosson merely set what he had: a "rough draft with many revisions, and a handwriting difficult to read."[17] Others believe that the manuscript was not in Shakespeare's and/or Wilkins' hand but was itself a pirated and poorly crafted reconstruction. Philip Edwards, for example, thinks it likely that Gosson's manuscript was put together by two reporters, one who worked on Acts 1-2, and a second who accounted for the rest of the play.[18] Gary Taylor speculates that the principal reporter was a boy actor who had played Marina, Lychorida, and Antiochus' daughter. The second reporter may have been the actor who had played a fisherman in Scene 2.1 and Pander in 4.2 and 4.6.[19] If so, the faults in the text have more to do with the memory of the boy actors than the legibility of the manuscript or the accuracy of the printhouse compositors. Without the original manuscript in hand, it is impossible to say whether the play's various textual difficulties stem from one or more of the following:

1. the carelessness of construction;

2. the difficulties of collaboration (particularly in regard to abridgement);

3. the illegibility of a rough manuscript;

4. the inaccuracy of memorial copyists (if there were any memorial copyists);

5. the inaccuracy of typesetters.

Despite these intractable difficulties, F.D. Hoeniger (Arden ed. 1963), Philip Edwards (Penguin ed. 1976), Gary Taylor (Oxford *Complete Works* ed. 1988) and Roger Warren (Oxford ed. 2003) have each attempted to mend some of *Pericles'* textual infirmities by borrowing from Wilkins' *Painfull Adventures of Pericles Prince of Tyre* (1608).[20] However, as the Norton editor Walter Cohen points out, the chances of a reconstructed text matching what Shakespeare actually wrote are about "nil."[21] I readily admit that there are brainteasers in *Pericles*; but I also submit that editors,

---

16   See Philip Edwards, New Penguin ed. 1976; rev.1996: 199-204; Gen. Eds. Wells and Taylor, *William Shakespeare: The Complete Works* (Oxford: Clarendon, 1988) 1037 and accompanying *Textual Companion* (Oxford: Clarendon, 1987), 556.

17   Stephen Orgel, *The Pelican Shakespeare* ed. 2001: XXXVII.

18   Philip Edwards, "An Approach to the Problem of *Pericles*," *Shakespeare Survey* 5 (1952): 25-49.

19   Gary Taylor, "The Transmission of *Pericles*," *Papers of the Bibliographical Society of America* 80 (1986), 193-217; esp.216; see also Roger Warren, Oxford ed., 2003: 79.

20   No doubt, all these editions were influenced by Kenneth Muir's *Shakespeare as Collaborator* (London: Methuen and Co., 196), esp. 60-65.

21   Walter Cohen, "A Reconstructed Text of *Pericles, Prince of Tyre*." *The Norton Shakespeare* (New York: Norton, 1997), 2709-2718; 2717. Even if we could solve these very serious issues of authorship and memorial reconstruction, we would still be faced with the problem of Wilkins' novelistic departures from the *Pericles* play. F.D. Hoeniger notes that Shakespeare's reliance on Twine as source for 4.1, 4.3 and 4.4; whereas in Wilkins' version Twine's novel accounts for about one-third of the entire story (Arden ed. 1963: XVI). See also Kenneth Muir, *The Painfull Adventures of Pericles, Prince of Tyre*, V, XII, 111-19. It is possible that Wilkins faithfully novelized an early and now lost version of the play, or that Wilkins, dissatisfied with Shakespeare's version, overturned him in the novelization.

no matter how ingenious, will not solve many of them. Consequently, this edition will favor a traditional text of *Pericles* on the belief that it is better to tweak obviously corrupted passages by Shakespeare than to pad out or to correct the play with intact but artistically inferior passages by Wilkins.

In Performance

In its own day, *Pericles* was among Shakespeare's most popular plays. It was performed at the Globe in 1607-08 and printed in quarto six times between 1609 and 1635 and revived for live performances in 1610, 1619 and 1631, yet, oddly, the play's performance history from the Restoration onward is unenviable. In 1659, the play was "highly applauded" but soon fell out of favor.[22] George Lillo adapted parts of *Pericles* into *Marina* (1738), but it was performed just three times, "owing to the lateness of the season and the weakness of the cast."[23]

Over the last 150 years or so, directors have abridged or bowdlerized the play with perhaps too free a hand. Samuel Phelps' 1854 production cut large sections of the text, including all the Chorus and brothel scenes, and filled the space with spectacular sets:

> When he [Pericles] sails at last to the temple of Diana of the Ephesians, rowers take their places on their banks, the vessel seems to glide along the coast, an admirably painted panorama slides before the eye, and the whole theatre seems to be in the course of actual transportation to the temple at Ephesus, which is the crowning scenic glory of the play. The dresses, too, are brilliant. As beseems an Eastern story, the events all pass among princes. Now the spectator has a scene presented to him occupied by characters who appear to have stepped out of a Greek vase; and presently he looks into an Assyrian palace and sees figures that have come to life and colour from the stones of Nineveh. There are noble banquets and glittering processions, and in the banquet-hall of King Simonides there is a dance which is a marvel of glitter, combinations of colour, and quaint picturesque effect. There are splendid trains of courtiers, there are shining rows of Vestal virgins, and there is Diana herself in the sky.[24]

Douglas Jarrold complained that the production rendered *Pericles* "a play more to be seen than heard."[25]

---

22   F.D. Hoeniger, Arden ed. 1963: LXVII.

23   Anonymous review, cited in David Skeele, *"Pericles* in Criticism and Production: A Brief History." *Pericles: Critical Essays* (London and New York: Garland Publishing, Inc, 2000), 1-33; 25.

24   W. May Phelps, Johnston Forbes-Robertson, *The Life and Life-Work of Samuel Phelps* (London: Sampson Low, Marston, Searle & Rivington, 1886), 142.

25   Douglas Jarrold quoted in J.R. Mulryne, "'To Glad Your Ear and Please Your Eye': *Pericles* at the Other Place [1979]." *Pericles: Critical Essays*, 288-96; 289.

On April 23, 1900, as part of a celebration of Shakespeare's birthday at Stratford-upon-Avon, director John Coleman staged the play but expunged the entire first act and all the brothel scenes in the fourth act.[26] Oscar Asche, who played Cleon in the production, called it a "disgraceful insult to the Bard."[27] But most critics and journalists thought that the cuts were necessary. Typical in this regard was Algernon Charles Swinburne, who felt only "repulsion" in reading the brothel scenes and assumed that his perceptions were shared by any "healthy-minded and reasonable human creature."[28]

A full text of *Pericles* was finally staged by Robert Atkins at the Old Vic in 1921. The restored incest and brothel scenes did little to change critical opinion. Edward Shanks called it "the best Shakespearean production I have seen for many years," but regretted that *Pericles* remained in his view "one of the worst plays that Shakespeare ever had anything to do with."[29] When the production was revived in 1939, Atkins added some ballet dancing, which seemed to mollify the reviewer for *The Observer*, who wrote: "Mr. Atkins produces the piece the only way now conceivable, as a fairy-tale, a Christmas mummery for midsummer nights."[30] In 1929, director Nugent Monck cut the incest scene (1.1), which he considered "pointless." He also added a sword dance, a number of songs, and a *Romeo-and-Juliet*-inspired balcony scene.[31] In 1947, Monck directed the play yet again and again cut the incest scene. This version began at 2.1 with a *Tempest*-like shipwreck. His rationale was not, however, to make any connection between *Pericles* and the late Romances but to "get the audience in and out and save on the electricity bills."[32] Director Tony Richardson (Old Vic production of 1957) revived Phelps' theatrical spectacle, which, in the words of one reviewer, made "it almost as difficult to follow the sense as the nonsense."[33]

In the last several decades, however, directors and critics have put aside much of Phelps' and Monck's gimmickry. Instead of elaborate sets and wild costumes, director Terry Hands (1969 Royal Shakespeare Company) opted for a virtually empty set, illumed with white light. Just as notably, Hands cast Susan Fleetwood

---

26   Gideon Lester, "The Triumph of *Pericles*." *ARTicles Online*. 1. 4b (June 2003). http://www.amrep.org/articles/1_4/triumph.html.

27   Oscar Asche, *Oscar Asche: His Life* (London: Hurst and Blackett, Ltd, [1929?]), 88.

28   Algernon Charles Swinburne, *A Study of Shakespeare*. Fifth impression (Rpt. New York: AMS, 1965), 208.

29   Edward Shanks, Review of Robert Atkins' *Pericles*, in *London Outlook*, May 21, 1921.

30   "*Pericles*: Partly By William Shakespeare." *The Observer*, June 25, 1945.

31   The play was performed by the Norwich Players. See Franklin J. Hildy, *Shakespeare at the Maddermarket: Nugent Monck and the Norwich Players* (Ann Arbor, Michigan: UNI Research Press, 1986), 116.

32   Micheline Steinberg, *Flashback : A Pictorial History, 1879-1979 : One Hundred Years of Stratford-upon-Avon and the Royal Shakespeare Company* (Stratford-upon-Avon: RSC Publications, 1985), 52,

33   Gideon Lester, "The Triumph of Pericles." *ARTicles Online*. 1. 4b (June 2003). http://www.amrep.org/articles/1_4/triumph.html.

as Thaisa *and* Marina. This doubling allowed audience members to follow visually and, more importantly, to bond emotionally with one actress through much of the play.[34] However John Barber was none-too-impressed with Ian Richardson's Pericles, whom he described as a "slight, forlorn creature without quite the presence of a fairy-tale hero."[35] Director Toby Robinson (Her Majesty's Theatre, 1973) set the play in a brothel and had it performed by actors who, for large measures of the show, paraded as drag queens. Despite a brilliant performance by Derek Jacobi as Pericles, critics variously argued that the production was either "too-ingenious" or just plain "disastrous."[36] There was no ballet or *Romeo*esque romance in Ron Daniel's 1979 production (RSC Other Place, Stratford-upon-Avon), which had the people of Tarsus dressed in rags, whimpering in pain and fear, and "evoking," in the words of R.R. Mulryne, "modern guilt over third world famine."[37]

Because of its widespread availability, many are familiar with the sadly lackluster BBC Shakespeare TV production of 1984. Despite the fact that much of the play takes place in port cities, director David Jones opted for a vaguely biblical desert. Juliet Stevenson played a convincing Thaisa but was on screen for only a handful of scenes and could not counter Edward Petherbridge's dreary Gower or Mike Gwilym's perpetually glum Pericles. Although Jones used Wilkins to fill in some dialogue at 4.6, he inserted entirely new lyrics for Marina's song in 5.1, composed by Martin Best.[38] Like all of the BBC Shakespeares, this *Pericles* was shot on video. As a consequence, its production values look distinctly low-budget. While some plays in the series are dramatically intense, this production seems rambling and disordered — not surprising, given that director David Jones thought of Pericles as dazed and confused, or as he put it, a "guy who gets hit over the head."[39]

In 1989, the RSC (dir. David Walker) staged a superb *Pericles*, starring Nigel Terry. Known to Americans as King Arthur in John Boorman's film *Excalibur*, Terry brought a mythic quality to the role. He was, however, injured during the production run and replaced by the far flatter Rob Edwards, who played the prince as if he were "a rational Jane Austen hero on a singularly unpropitious tour of the

---

34   Terry Hands' production also anticipated Gary Taylor's textual approach. Hands added some 34 lines from Wilkins' *The Painfull Adventures of Pericles Prince of Tyre* to Act 4.6. See J.R. Mulryne, "'To Glad Your Ear and Please Your Eye': *Pericles* at the Other Place [1979]," 291.

35   See David Skeele, *Thwarting the Wayward Seas: A Critical and Theatrical History of Shakespeare's Pericles in the Nineteenth and Twentieth Centuries* (Newark, DE: University of Delaware Press, 1998), 118.

36   John Barber, "Curious trappings in 'Pericles.'" *The Daily Telegraph*, August 22, 1973; Irving Wardle, "Pericles," *The Times*, August 28, 1973.

37   J.R. Mulryne, "'To Glad Your Ear and Please Your Eye': *Pericles* at the Other Place [1979]," 293.

38   Paul Nelson, "Shot from the Canon: The BBC Video of *Pericles*." *Pericles: Critical Essays*, 297-324; 312, 315, 324 n.33.

39   Laurie E. Maguire, *Studying Shakespeare: A Guide to the Plays* (Oxford: Blackwell Publishing, 2004), 218.

Levant."[40] In 1993, the company Wooden Tongues staged an unusual *Pericles* which included a seven-foot-high puppet in the role of Antiochus, and two Aunt Sally caricatures as Bawd and Boult.[41] Even more oddly, Marina doubled with Gower, who "gesture[d] like an android when narrating."[42] In a 2003 production (Lyric Hammersmith) director Neil Bartlett staged the play as if it were the dream of a mental patient. A joint effort by the Royal Shakespeare Company and Cardboard Citizens (dir. Adrian Jackson, 2003)—the latter, a theatre company that works on site-specific productions with homeless people and refugees—featured:

> interwoven verbatim accounts of modern refugee experiences. …
> A mother recalls fleeing her country and being aboard a packed
> sinking boat with three women going into labor. A corpse, she
> says, float[ed] past her with its baby umbilically attached.[43]

While attempts to make *Pericles* more relevant are to be applauded, critics found this particular production too earnestly political. *The Telegraph*'s Dominic Cavendish described the show as initially "intimidating then extensively dull"; *The Guardian*'s Michael Billington agreed: "I found the three-hour show something to be endured more than enjoyed."[44]

Yet other directors have tried to lighten the tragedy of the play with a catwalk of costume. In a 1994 production at the National Theatre (dir. Phyllida Lloyd), actors paraded the stage in Eskimo, Incan, and ancient Assyrian costumes. The production was glibly dismissed by Charles Spencer as "Shakespeare in silly hats."[45] A recent RSC (2006) production directed by Dominic Cooke, recast the play to reflect the ongoing political struggles in Zimbabwe—with the incestuous and tyrannous Antiochus (Clarence Smith) looking and sounding like Robert Mugabe—but it also included a fair amount of carnival: a Soho pole-dancing club represented the brothel in Mytilene; a London inhabited by a "New Age healer and Cockney hoodies" represented Ephesus; the tournament in which Pericles wins Thaisa included "a spoof steeplechase and a parody of Olympic swimming."[46] While Shakespeare's tragedies almost always have at least one scene of merriment amid the murk of misfortune, comic transformations in *Pericles*, at least for those unfamiliar

40   Michael Billington, "Pericles reborn." *The Guardian*, April 14, 1990.

41   An Aunt Sally is a traditional British figurine of an old woman with a pipe.

42   Nick Curtis, "Lifeless resurrections." *The Independent*, October 13, 1993.

43   Kate Bassett, "All washed up (on a shore of wet jumpers)." *Independent on Sunday*, August 3, 2003.

44   Dominic Cavendish, "A punishing, purgatorial meander with Pericles." *Telegraph*, July 28, 2003; Michael Billington, "Seeking asylum in Shakespeare." *The Guardian*, July 28, 2003.

45   Charles Spencer, "Shakespeare in silly hats." *Daily Telegraph*, May 23, 1994.

46   See Ian Shuttleworth, "*The Winter's Tale/Pericles*." *Financial Times*, November 17, 2006; Benedict Nightingale, "*The Winter's Tale/Pericles*." *The Times*, November 17, 2006.

with its performance history, run the danger of making the play "seem even more preposterous than it is."[47]

Though many of these productions have shined a light on the brilliance of a scene or character in the play, no one production has yet to redeem fully *Pericles'* blighted performance history. Through no fault of its own, the play has endured mishaps in print and in performance. For the first four acts of the play, Prince Pericles wanders impoverished and forlorn; we can only hope that the right combination of talent and circumstance will finally afford the play that happy fifth act which Shakespeare envisioned for its hero.

Jeffrey Kahan, ULV

---

47   Benedict Nightingale, "*Pericles*, Lyric Hammersmith." *The Times*, September 26, 2003.

PERICLES, PRINCE OF TYRE

DRAMATIS PERSONAE

Gower, as Chorus.

Antiochus, King of Antioch.
Pericles, Prince of Tyre.
Helicanus, } two lords of Tyre.
Escanes,
Simonides, King of Pentapolis.
Cleon, Governor of Tharsus.
Lysimachus, Governor of Mytilene.
Cerimon, a lord of Ephesus.
Thaliard, a lord of Antioch.
Philemon, servant to *Cerimon.*
Leonine, servant to *Dionyza.*
Marshal.

A Pander.
Boult, his servant.

The Daughter of *Antiochus.*
Dionyza, wife to *Cleon.*
Thaisa, daughter to *Simonides.*
Marina, daughter to *Pericles* and *Thaisa.*
Lychorida, nurse to *Marina.*
A Bawd.

Diana.

Lords, Ladies, Knights, Gentlemen,
Sailors, Pirates, Fishermen, Messengers.

SCENE.—*In various countries.*

1

Act I

Enter Gower.[†]

[*Antioch. Before the Palace of Antiochus.*]

To sing a song that old was sung,
From ashes ancient Gower is come,
Assuming man's infirmities
To glad your ear and please your eyes.
It hath been sung at festivals,   5
On ember-eves and holy-ales;
And lords and ladies in their lives
Have read it for restoratives.
The purchase is to make men glorious,
Et bonum quo antiquius, eo melius.   10
If you, born in these latter times
When wit's more ripe, accept my rhymes,
And that to hear an old man sing
May to your wishes pleasure bring,
I life would wish, and that I might   15
Waste it for you, like taper light.

Prologue
References to the *Pericles* story as found in Gower, Twine, and Wilkins are derived from Geoffrey Bullough, *Narrative and Dramatic Sources of Shakespeare*. 8. vols. (London, Routledge and Kegan Paul; New York, Columbia University Press, 1957-75), Vol. VI. References to Wilkins' *The Miseries of Enforced Marriage* are derived from a diplomatic transcription prepared by Glenn H. Blayney for Oxford University Press/The Malone Society Reprints, 1964. 2. **Gower:** John Gower, fourteenth-century poet. —**come:** The eighteenth-century editor George Steevens suggested *sprung*. 3. **Assuming man's infirmities:** ie. Gower's spirit assuming corporeal form. 6. **ember-eves...holy-ales:** holidays, the former a Christian period of fasting. 8. **restoratives:** ie. a feel-good story, one that cheers and, thus, renews. 9. **purchase:** gain; Malone emended to *purpose*. 10. *Et bonum quo antiquius, eo melius:* Latin. The more ancient a thing, the better. 12. **ripe:** sophisticated. 13. **that to hear:** if to hear. 15-16. **I life would wish, and that I might/Waste it for you, like taper light:** Roughly, if my life were a candle, I could only wish to dazzle you with the incandescence of my tale.

[†]   For director David Thacker's 1990 RSC production, a bow-tied Rudolph Walker good-humouredly pointed to a red, leather bound book when affirming the ludicrous details of the story (C.S. "Pericles's great voyage of discovery." *The Daily Telegraph*. April 14, 1990). In director Phyllida Lloyd's 1994 production at the National Theatre, Gower (Henry Goodman) sprang out of a piano with a "jack-in-the-box spring" (Paul Taylor, "Under the weather." *The Independent*, May 24, 1994). In 2002 production by the London Bubble (Chiswick House grounds), "Gower happily dominates the evening. Like a master of ceremonies, he whips the pace along whenever the text shows severe signs of sagging" (Rachel Halliburton, "Putting panto into Pericles." *Evening Standard*, August 1, 2002). In Neil Bartlett's 2003 Lyric Hammersmith production, Bette Bourne's Gower was "a shambling old caretaker in a brown coat" (Benedict Nightingale, *Pericles*, Lyric Hammersmith." *The Times*, September 26, 2003).

A bow-tied Rudolph Walker as Gower. *Pericles*, 1989, directed by David Thacker, designed by Fran Thompson. (Joe Cocks Studio Collection © Shakespeare Birthplace Trust)

This Antioch, then, Antiochus the Great
Built up, this city, for his chiefest seat,
The fairest in all Syria—
I tell you what mine authors say.   20
This king unto him took a peer,
Who died and left a female heir,
So buxom, blithe, and full of face
As heaven had lent her all his grace;
With whom the father liking took   25
And her to incest did provoke.
Bad child; worse father! to entice his own
To evil should be done by none.
By custom what they did begin
Was with long use account'd no sin.   30
The beauty of this sinful dame
Made many princes thither frame,

18. **chiefest seat:** the capitol. 20. **I tell you what mine authors say:** suggesting that Gower himself is borrowing from a still older text. 21. **peer:** mate; Kittredge printed *feere*, perhaps combining Theobald's *pheere* and Dyce's reading of *fere*, meaning companion. Neither word suggests the incestuous nature of the relationship. 23. **buxom, blithe, and full of face:** lively, care-free, perfectly featured. 24. **heaven:** ie. God. 26. **provoke:** Note, however, that Shakespeare's Gower also blames the child in line 27. This differs from Gower's original tale, in which it is clear that Antiochus rapes his daughter: "And she was tender, and full of drede,/ She couth nought hir maydenhede/ Defende" (*Confessio Amantis*, BK VIII: 309-312). 28. **To evil:** to commit evil. 30. **with long use account'd no sin:** ie. incest became natural to them, though this is countered by Antiochus' terror that his secret affair will be made public. 32. **frame:** go.

> To seek her as a bedfellow,
> In marriage pleasures playfellow;
> Which to prevent he made a law—   35
> To keep her still, and men in awe—
> That whoso ask'd her for his wife,
> His riddle told not, lost his life.
> So for her many a wight did die,
> As yon grim looks do testify.   40
> What now ensues, to the judgment of your eye
> I give, my cause who best can justify.   *Exit.*

SCENE I. [*Antioch. A room in the Palace.*]†

Enter Antiochus, Prince Pericles, and Followers.

ANTIOCHUS   Young Prince of Tyre, you have at large receiv'd
The danger of the task you undertake.

PERICLES   I have, Antiochus, and, with a soul
Embold'ned with the glory of her praise,
Think death no hazard in this enterprise.   *Music.*   5

---

33. **bedfellow:** companion, often assigned to men; the following line suggests sexual partner. 38. **His riddle told not:** failed to solve the riddle. 39. **wight:** person. 40. **As yon grim looks:** Likely a prop reference—ie. a series of heads on sticks or on the battlements of the palace.
SCENE I.
1. **at large receiv'd:** fully heard.

---

†   In 1973, director Toby Robertson (Prospect Theatre Company) staged the play as an entertainment performed within the Mytilene brothel. Despite a brilliant performance by Derek Jacobi as Pericles, the production was deemed by critics as either "too-ingenious"(John Barber, "Curious trappings in 'Pericles.'" *The Daily Telegraph*, August 22, 1973) or as just plain "disastrous" (Irving Wardle, "Pericles," *The Times*, August 28, 1973). A 2002 RSC production at the Roundhouse Theatre (dir. Adrian Noble), opened "on a stage full of stunning lanterns and a heady scent of incense" (Jenny Dormer, *Stratford Standard*, August 16, 2002); Susannah Clapp, however, registered an entirely different impression: "a chamber of horrors—severed heads swing like conkers on long ropes" (*Observer*, July 14, 2002). Neil Bartlett's 2003 Lyric Hammersmith production set the play in a hospital/insane asylum, with swing doors, oxygen tanks. Pericles wandered "forlornly round the stage in pajamas and moth-eaten cardigan" (Charles Spencer, "Moving from the ridiculous to the sublime" (*The Daily Telegraph*, September 29, 2003). A (RSC/Cardboard Citizens, 2003) production directed by Adrian Jackson recast the play to reflect the ongoing dilemma of political refugees: "In one huge chamber, you sit at shabby desks and are told to fill in a seemingly endless Home Office form, which made me want to cry almost instantly. In another, child-size camp beds stretch out to the crack of doom in the half-dark. Mountains of second-hand clothes are piled in corners and inside a bunch of canvas tents, television monitors flicker, showing real-life immigrants telling their stories" (Kate Bassett, "All washed up (on a shore of wet jumpers)." *Independent on Sunday*, August 3, 2003). A recent RSC (2006) production directed by Dominic Cooke recast the play to reflect ongoing political struggles in Africa, the tyrannous Antiochus (Clarence Smith) looking and sounding like Robert Mugabe (Ian Shuttleworth, "The Winter's Tale/Pericles." *Financial Times*, November, 17, 2006).

ANTIOCHUS	Bring in our daughter, clothed like a bride
	For the embracements even of Jove himself;
	At whose conception, till Lucina reign'd,
	Nature this dowry gave to glad her presence,
	The senate house of planets all did sit 10
	To knit in her their best perfections.

Enter Antiochus' Daughter.‡

PERICLES	See where she comes, apparell'd like the spring,
	Graces her subjects, and her thoughts the king
	Of every virtue gives renown to men!
	Her face the book of praises, where is read 15
	Nothing but curious pleasures, as from thence
	Sorrow were ever ras'd, and testy wrath
	Could never be her mild companion.
	You gods that made me man, and sway in love,
	That have inflam'd desire in my breast 20
	To taste the fruit of yon celestial tree
	Or die in the adventure, be my helps,
	As I am son and servant to your will,
	To compass such a boundless happiness!
ANTIOCHUS	Prince Pericles— 25
PERICLES	That would be son to great Antiochus.
ANTIOCHUS	Before thee stands this fair Hesperides,
	With golden fruit, but dangerous to be touch'd;
	For death, like dragons, here affright the hoard.
	Her face, like heaven, enticeth thee to view 30

---

7. **embracements even of Jove himself:** Jove, or Zeus in the Greek, often selected the most beautiful mortals for dalliances. Since Jove married his sister, Juno, Antiochus may also be hinting at his incestuous desires here. 8. **Lucina:** goddess of childbirth. 10-11. **senate house of planets all did sit/To knit in her their best perfections:** Roughly, the stars have aligned to create her beauty. 12. **apparell'd like the spring:** fresh, fertile, blooming. 15. **book of praises:** memorable praises. 17. **ras'd:** erased. —**testy:** irritable, touchy. **You gods that...sway in love:** Cupid or his mother Venus. 21-22. **the fruit ...Or die:** Woman as fruit; Eve ate the apple and brought sin into the world. 24. **To compass:** To accomplish; achieve. 27. **Hesperides:** In Greek myth, daughters of the Titan Atlas and Hesperis, who guarded the golden apples; often associated with a garden of heavenly bliss; Elysium.

---

‡   The 1984 BBC production had Antiochus (John Woodvine) and his daughter (Edita Brychta) French kissing matter-of-factly. For director Simon Usher's 1990 Leicester Haymarket production, Valerie Gogan played Antiochus' daughter as a "pitiable anorexic victim" (Paul Taylor, "A family business." *The Independent*, March 15, 1990); whereas Sarah McVicar, playing the same role for the RSC (David Thacker dir., 1990), shamelessly and happily hugged her father and flirted with Nigel Terry's Pericles.

Her countless glory, which desert must gain;
And which, without desert because their eye
Presumes to reach, all this whole heap must die.
Yon sometime famous princes, like thyself,
Drawn by report, advent'rous by desire,   35
Tell thee, with speechless tongues and semblance pale,
That, without covering, save yon field of stars,
Here they stand martyrs slain in Cupid's wars;
And with dead cheeks advise thee to desist
For going on death's net, whom none resist.   40

PERICLES   Antiochus, I thank thee, who hast taught
My frail mortality to know itself,
And by those fearful objects to prepare
This body, like to them, to what I must;
For death remembered should be like a mirror,   45
Who tells us life's but breath, to trust it error.
I'll make my will then, and, as sick men do,
Who know the world, see heaven, but, feeling woe,
Gripe not at earthly joys as erst they did,
So I bequeath a happy peace to you   50
And all good men, as every prince should do;
My riches to the earth, from whence they came;
But my unspotted fire of love to you.   [*To the Princess.*]
Thus ready for the way of life or death,
I wait the sharpest blow, Antiochus.   55

ANTIOCHUS   Scorning advice, read the conclusion then;
Which read and not expounded, 'tis decreed,
As these before thee, thou thyself shalt bleed.

DAUGHTER   Of all 'say'd yet, mayst thou prove prosperous!
Of all 'say'd yet, I wish thee happiness!   60

PERICLES   Like a bold champion I assume the lists,
Nor ask advice of any other thought
But faithfulness and courage.   [*Reads.*]
The Riddle.
    'I am no viper, yet I feed
    On mother's flesh which did me breed.   65

---

31. **desert:** deserving. 34. **Yon sometime famous princes:** the skulls of prior suitors; see Prologue 40, above. 38. **martyrs slain in Cupid's wars:** died, sacrificed for love. 45-46. **death remembered should be like a mirror,/Who tells us life's but breath, to trust it error:** Difficult. Perhaps, mirrors do not reflect reality; physical life is only a semblance of real, immortal life. 49. **Gripe not...as erst they did:** Do not grasp as they did before. 50. **So I bequeath a happy peace to you:** Roughly, if I die, do not feel guilty. 52. **riches:** body. 59. **prosperous:** successful. 61. **the lists:** challenge, often associated with chivalric duels.

Pericles, 1958, directed by Tony Richardson, designed by Loudon Sainthill. The photograph shows Antiochus (Paul Hardwick, left) intimidating his daughter (Zoe Caldwell). (Angus McBean © Royal Shakespeare Company)

I sought a husband, in which labor
I found that kindness in a father.
He's father, son, and husband mild;
I mother, wife, and yet his child.
How they may be, and yet in two,   70
As you will live, resolve it you.'

Sharp physic is the last! but, O you powers
That give heaven countless eyes to view men's acts,
Why cloud they not their sights perpetually
If this be true which makes me pale to read it?   75
Fair glass of light, I lov'd you, and could still,
Were not this glorious casket stor'd with ill.
But I must tell you, now my thoughts revolt;
For he's no man on whom perfections wait
That, knowing sin within, will touch the gate.   80

---

72. **Sharp physic:** distasteful medicine; physically painful, ill news. 74. **Why cloud they not their sights:** Roughly, why don't the gods hide this sin? 76. **Fair glass of light:** A reference to her seeming purity; like a mirror, she reflects light/goodness, but does not contain it. 77. **glorious casket:** looks are deceiving.

Y'are a fair viol, and your sense the strings;
Who, finger'd to make man his lawful music,
Would draw heaven down, and all the gods, to hearken;
But being play'd upon before your time,
Hell only danceth at so harsh a chime.   85
Good sooth, I care not for you.

ANTIOCHUS   Prince Pericles, touch not, upon thy life,
For that's an article within our law,
As dangerous as the rest. Your time's expir'd.
Either expound now, or receive your sentence.   90

PERICLES   Great king,
Few love to hear the sins they love to act.
'Twould braid yourself too near for me to tell it.
Who has a book of all that monarchs do,
He's more secure to keep it shut than shown;   95
For vice repeated is like the wand'ring wind,
Blows dust in others' eyes, to spread itself;
And yet the end of all is bought thus dear,
The breath is gone, and the sore eyes see clear
To stop the air would hurt them. The blind mole casts   100
Copp'd hills towards heaven, to tell the earth is throng'd
By man's oppression, and the poor worm doth die for't.
Kings are earth's gods; in vice their law's their will;
And if Jove stray, who dares say Jove doth ill?
It is enough you know; and it is fit,   105
What being more known grows worse, to smother it.
All love the womb that their first being bred,
Then give my tongue like leave to love my head.

ANTIOCHUS   [Aside.] Heaven, that I had thy head!
He has found the meaning.   110
But I will gloze with him.—Young Prince of Tyre,
Though by the tenour of our strict edíct,
Your exposition misinterpreting,
We might proceed to cancel off your days,
Yet hope, succeeding from so fair a tree   115

81-85. fair viol... harsh a chime: The instrument, her body, has been ruined by ill-use. 87. touch not: See Antiochus' injunction at 1.1.28. 90. expound: explain. 93. braid: upbraid. 94-95. Who has a book ...keep it shut than shown: hide your secret. 100-102. mole...worm: Moles, with their fortress-like hills, dine on worms; compared to powerful kings who oppress common men. A similar image is used at 2.1.27. 108. Then give my tongue like leave to love my head: Roughly, I'd rather keep the secret than lose my head. 109. that I had thy head: a reason to execute him. 111. gloze: speak kindly; here meant duplicitously.

As your fair self, doth tune us otherwise.
Forty days longer we do respite you;
If by which time our secret be undone,
This mercy shows we'll joy in such a son;
And until then your entertain shall be   120
As doth befit our honor and your worth.

All Exit. Pericles Remains.

PERICLES   How courtesy would seem to cover sin,
When what is done is like an hypocrite,
The which is good in nothing but in sight!
If it be true that I interpret false,   125
Then were it certain you were not so bad
As with foul incest to abuse your soul;
Where now you're both a father and a son
By your untimely claspings with your child
(Which pleasures fit a husband, not a father),   130
And she an eater of her mother's flesh
By the defiling of her parents' bed;
And both like serpents are, who though they feed
On sweetest flowers, yet they poison breed.
Antioch, farewell! for wisdom sees, those men   135
Blush not in actions blacker than the night,
Will shun no course to keep them from the light.
One sin, I know, another doth provoke;
Murther's as near to lust as flame to smoke.
Poison and treason are the hands of sin;   140
Ay, and the targets to put off the shame.
Then, lest my life be cropp'd to keep you clear,
By flight I'll shun the danger which I fear.   *Exit.*

Enter Antiochus.

ANTIOCHUS   He hath found the meaning, for the which we mean
To have his head.   145
He must not live to trumpet forth my infamy,
Nor tell the world Antiochus doth sin
In such a loathed manner;
And therefore instantly this prince must die;

---

116. **tune:** importune, beg. Antiochus echoes Pericles' musical imagery of 1.1.81-85, above. 118. **undone:** solved. 128. **son:** In this instance, son-in-law. 129. **untimely:** unlucky, ill-fated, perhaps also playing on 1.1.81-85, as in musical time. 131. **an eater of her mother's flesh:** Difficult. Perhaps the child feeds on the pleasure reserved for its mother. 134. **poison breed:** Satan, as a snake, bought sin into the world. 137. **Will shun no course to keep them from the light:** Will do anything to keep their secrets. 141. **targets:** shields. 142. **cropp'd:** chopped—ie. beheaded. 148. **loathed:** loathsome. 149. **instantly:** on the instant.

For by his fall my honor must keep high.   150
Who attends us there?†

Enter Thaliard.

THALIARD   Doth your Highness call?

ANTIOCHUS   Thaliard,
You are of our chamber, Thaliard, and our mind partakes
Her private actions to your secrecy;
And for your faithfulness we will advance you.   155
Thaliard, behold, here's poison, and here's gold.
We hate the Prince of Tyre, and thou must kill him.
It fits thee not to ask the reason why.
Because we bid it. Say, is it done?

THALIARD   My lord, 'tis done.   160

Enter a Messenger.

ANTIOCHUS   Enough.—
Let your breath cool yourself, telling your haste.

MESSENGER   My lord, Prince Pericles is fled.   [*Exit.*]

ANTIOCHUS   As thou
Wilt live, fly after; and, like an arrow shot
From a well-experienc'd archer hits the mark   165
His eye doth level at, so thou ne'er return
Unless thou say Prince Pericles is dead.

THALIARD   My lord,
If I can get him within my pistol's length,
I'll make him sure enough. So farewell to your Highness.   170

ANTIOCHUS   Thaliard, adieu! [*Exit Thaliard.*] Till Pericles be dead
My heart can lend no succour to my head.   *Exit.*

---

153. **chamber:** inner council. 154. **Her:** the court, Antiochus' government. 156. **poison...gold:** In Gower, Thaliard, therein named Taliart, is a counselor to the King, not merely a hired henchman. 169. **pistol's length:** gun barrel's sight. 172. **succour:** relief.

---

†   In a 1996 production (Riverside Studios, London), dir. James Roose-Evans had Antiochus engaged not only in incest but also in a sexual relationship with Thaliard (Robert Hanks. "Pericles." *The Independent,* November 11, 1996).

SCENE II. [*Tyre. The Palace.*]

Enter Pericles with his Lords.

PERICLES   Let none disturb us.   [*Exeunt Lords.*]
            Why should this charge of thought,
            The sad companion, dull-ey'd melancholy,
            Be my so us'd a guest as not an hour
            In the day's glorious walk or peaceful night,   5
            The tomb where grief should sleep, can breed me quiet?
            Here pleasures court mine eyes, and mine eyes shun them,
            And danger, which I feared, is at Antioch,
            Whose arm seems far too short to hit me here.
            Yet neither pleasure's art can joy my spirits,   10
            Nor yet the other's distance comfort me.
            Then it is thus: the passions of the mind,
            That have their first conception by misdread,
            Have after-nourishment and life by care;
            And what was first but fear what might be done,   15
            Grows elder now, and cares it be not done.
            And so with me. The great Antiochus—
            'Gainst whom I am too little to contend,
            Since he's so great can make his will his act,
            Will think me speaking, though I swear to silence;   20
            Nor boots it me to say I honor him
            If he suspect I may dishonor him.
            And what may make him blush in being known,
            He'll stop the course by which it might be known.
            With hostile forces he'll o'erspread the land,   25
            And with th' ostent of war will look so huge
            Amazement shall drive courage from the state,
            Our men be vanquish'd ere they do resist,
            And subjects punish'd that ne'er thought offence;
            Which care of them, not pity of myself—   30

SCENE II.
3-9. **sad companion…Antioch…to hit me here:** Pericles expresses his state of depression and his fear of Antiochus. 12-15. **the passions of the mind…cares it be not done:** Roughly, fear takes on a life of its own. 18. **too little to contend:** Pericles' kingdom of Tyre is too weak geopolitically to deal with great and far-reaching Antioch; contradicted at 1.2.11, however. 21. **Nor boots it:** It doesn't matter. 24. **course:** discourse and the coursing of Pericles' blood, playing on *blush* in the previous line. 26. **ostent:** display.

Who am no more but as the tops of trees,
Which fence the roots they grow by and defend them—
Makes both my body pine and soul to languish,
And punish that before that he would punish.

Enter [Helicanus and] all the Lords to Pericles.

1. LORD   Joy and all comfort in your sacred breast!   35

2. LORD   And keep your mind, till you return to us,
Peaceful and comfortable!

HELICANUS   Peace, peace, and give experience tongue!
They do abuse the king that flatter him.
For flattery is the bellows blows up sin;   40
The thing the which is flattered, but a spark
To which that blast gives heat and stronger glowing;
Whereas reproof, obedient and in order,
Fits kings as they are men, for they may err.
When Signior Sooth here does proclaim a peace,   45
He flatters you, makes war upon your life.
Prince, pardon me; or strike me, if you please.
I cannot be much lower than my knees.   [*Kneels.*]

PERICLES   All leave us else; but let your cares o'erlook
What shipping and what lading's in our haven,   50
And then return to us. [*Exeunt Lords.*] Helicanus, thou
Hast moved us. What seest thou in our looks?

HELICANUS   An angry brow, dread lord.

PERICLES   If there be such a dart in princes' frowns,
How durst thy tongue move anger to our face?   55

HELICANUS   How dare the plants look up to heaven, from whence
They have their nourishment?

PERICLES   Thou know'st I have power
To take thy life from thee.

31-32. **as the tops of trees,/Which fence the roots they grow by and defend them:** Echoing George Wilkins' *Miseries of an Enforced Marriage* (1607): "Men must be like the branch and barke to trees,/ Which does defend them from tempestuous rage" (lines 269-270). 32. **fence the roots:** defense of the roots. 33. **pine:** pain and, possibly, to a pine tree. 34.*sd.* **Helicanus:** In Gower, Helicanus, there named Hellican, is not a counselor, but a loyal citizen who he meets on his return to Tyre. 38. **give experience tongue:** speak plainly and with wisdom, not with flattery. 40. **bellows:** A device that produces a strong current of air. Related to hellfire—hence, sin. 42. **blast gives heat and stronger glowing:** Bellows were used to heat coals; here meant to suggest that flattery blazes the worst aspects of power. 45. **Signior Sooth:** a typical flattering courtier, a yes-man. 50. **haven:** port. 56-57. **How dare the plants look up to heaven, from whence/ They have their nourishment:** Roughly, how can I give bad advice to the person on whom we all depend?

HELICANUS	I have ground the axe myself.	60
	Do but you strike the blow.	
PERICLES	Rise, prithee, rise. [*He rises.*]	
	Sit down. Thou art no flatterer.	
	I thank thee for't; and heaven forbid	
	That kings should let their ears hear their faults hid!	
	Fit counsellor and servant for a prince,	65
	Who by thy wisdom makes a prince thy servant,	
	What wouldst thou have me do?	
HELICANUS	To bear with patience	
	Such griefs as you yourself do lay upon yourself.	
PERICLES	Thou speak'st like a physician, Helicanus,	
	That ministers a potion unto me	70
	That thou wouldst tremble to receive thyself.	
	Attend me then. I went to Antioch,	
	Where, as thou know'st, against the face of death	
	I sought the purchase of a glorious beauty,	
	From whence an issue I might propagate	75
	Are arms to princes and bring joys to subjects.	
	Her face was to mine eye beyond all wonder;	
	The rest (hark in thine ear) as black as incest;	
	Which by my knowledge found, the sinful father	
	Seem'd not to strike, but smooth. But thou know'st this,	80
	'Tis time to fear when tyrants seem to kiss.	
	Which fear so grew in me I hither fled	
	Under the covering of a careful night,	
	Who seem'd my good protector; and being here,	
	Bethought me what was past, what might succeed.	85
	I knew him tyrannous; and tyrants' fears	
	Decrease not, but grow faster than the years;	
	And should he doubt it, as no doubt he doth,	
	That I should open to the list'ning air	
	How many worthy princes' bloods were shed	90
	To keep his bed of blackness unlaid ope,	

---

67. **What wouldst thou have me do:** Pericles' question signals that he is no tyrant. 69-70. **physician .... potion:** healing words, playing upon *Sharp physic* at 1.1.72. 73. **against the face of death:** on the possibility of death. 76. **Are arms:** There may be some missing text here, but the sense is that children would be a strength to the kingdom. 78. **black as incest:** sinful, though why it is *as* incest, rather than *due to* incest is not entirely clear. 81. **'Tis time to fear when tyrants seem to kiss:** This explains Pericles' fear when dealing with Simonides in 2.5. 83. **careful:** protecting; see next line. 86. **I knew him tyrannous:** Why Pericles would seek to marry into this family is not explained. 90-91. **How many worthy princes' bloods were shed/To keep his bed of blackness:** On the assumption that all other princes before him have also solved the riddle.

To lop that doubt, he'll fill this land with arms
And make pretence of wrong that I have done him;
When all, for mine, if I may call offence,
Must feel war's blow, who spares not innocence;   95
Which love to all, of which thyself art one,
Who now reprov'd'st me for't—

HELICANUS   Alas, sir!

PERICLES   Drew sleep out of mine eyes, blood from my cheeks,
Musings into my mind, with thousand doubts
How I might stop this tempest ere it came;   100
And finding little comfort to relieve them,
I thought it princely charity to grieve them.

HELICANUS   Well, my lord, since you have given me leave to speak,
Freely will I speak. Antiochus you fear,
And justly too I think you fear the tyrant,   105
Who either by public war or private treason
Will take away your life.
Therefore, my lord, go travel for a while,
Till that his rage and anger be forgot,
Or till the Destinies do cut his thread of life.   110
Your rule direct to any; if to me,
Day serves not light more faithful than I'll be.

PERICLES   I do not doubt thy faith;
But should he wrong my liberties in my absence?

HELICANUS   We'll mingle our bloods together in the earth,   115
From whence we had our being and our birth.

PERICLES   Tyre, I now look from thee then and to Tharsus
Intend my travel, where I'll hear from thee;
And by whose letters I'll dispose myself.
The care I had and have of subjects' good   120
On thee I lay, whose wisdom's strength can bear it.
I'll take thy word for faith, not ask thine oath.
Who shuns not to break one will sure crack both:

---

92. **To lop that doubt, he'll fill this land with arms:** Pun. His armies will lop off his enemies' arms.
An image of castration? To remain potent, Antiochus must emasculate his enemies' extremities. 95.
blow: violence. 98-100. **Drew sleep out...How I might stop this:** Roughly, I have been thinking long
and hard how to avoid bringing war to Tyre. 102. **to grieve them:** to grieve for them. 103. **leave:**
permission. 110. **Destinies do cut his thread of life:** Three Greek goddesses: Clothio spins the thread
of life, another, Lahesis, measures its length, and a third, Atropos, cuts it off. 114. **wrong my liberties:**
invade my provinces. 116. **we had our being and our birth:** In Greek myth, as in Christianity, man was
formed of the earth. Prometheus formed man out of mud; Athena then breathed life into the clay. 122.
I'll take thy word for faith, not ask thine oath: The loyalty of Helicanus is a repeated motif. See 2.4.

But in our orbs we'll live so round and safe
That time of both this truth shall ne'er convince,   125
Thou show'dst a subject's shine, I a true prince.   *Exeunt.*

Scene III. [*Tyre. The Palace.*]

Enter Thaliard solus.

THALIARD   So, this is Tyre, and this the court. Here must I kill King Pericles;
and if I do it not, I am sure to be hang'd at home. 'Tis dangerous.
Well, I perceive he was a wise fellow and had good discretion that,
being bid to ask what he would of the king, desired he might know
none of his secrets. Now do I see he had some reason for't; for if a
king bid a man be a villain, he's bound by the indenture of his oath
to be one. Husht! here comes the lords of Tyre.   7

Enter Helicanus, Escanes, with other Lords.

HELICANUS   You shall not need, my fellow peers of Tyre,
Further to question me of your king's departure.
His seal'd commission, left in trust with me,
Does speak sufficiently he's gone to travel.   10

THALIARD   [*Aside.*] How? the King gone?

HELICANUS   If further yet you will be satisfied
Why (as it were unlicens'd of your loves)
He would depart, I'll give some light unto you.   15
Being at Antioch—

THALIARD   [*Aside.*]   What from Antioch?

HELICANUS   Royal Antiochus, on what cause I know not,
Took some displeasure at him; at least he judg'd so;
And doubting lest that he had err'd or sinn'd,
To show his sorrow, he'd correct himself;   20
So puts himself unto the shipman's toil,
With whom each minute threatens life or death.

---

124. **our orbs:** our orbits; the planets were each thought to represent self-contained personality traits.
Pericles suggests that he and Helicanus will maintain order by being true to their respective natures.
Scene III.
1. **So, this is Tyre, and this the court:** This exposition is common in Shakespeare and replaces
inordinate stage scenery. 10. **seal'd commission:** an authorizing stamp. 14. **unlicens'd of your loves:**
Done without your direct permission. Note the difference in regimes. Pericles treats his lords as equals or
even as his masters; Antiochus merely terrorizes his subjects. 15. **light:** enlighten, inform. 21. **shipman's
toil:** the rigors of the sea.

THALIARD	[*Aside.*] Well, I perceive	
	I shall not be hang'd now, although I would;	
	But since he's gone, the King's ears it must please	25
	He scap'd the land to perish on the seas.	
	I'll present myself.—Peace to the lords of Tyre!	
HELICANUS	Lord Thaliard from Antiochus is welcome.	
THALIARD	From him I come	
	With message unto princely Pericles;	30
	But since my landing I have understood	
	Your lord has betook himself to unknown travels.	
	Now message must return from whence it came.	
HELICANUS	We have no reason to desire it,	
	Commended to our master, not to us.	35
	Yet, ere you shall depart, this we desire—	
	As friends to Antioch, we may feast in Tyre. *Exeunt.*	

SCENE IV. [*Tharsus. The Governor's house.*]

Enter Cleon, the Governor of Tharsus, with his wife [Dionyza] and Others.

CLEON	My Dionyza, shall we rest us here,	
	And by relating tales of others' griefs,	
	See if 'twill teach us to forget our own?	
DIONYZA	That were to blow at fire in hope to quench it;	
	For who digs hills because they do aspire	5
	Throws down one mountain to cast up a higher.	
	O my distressed lord, even such our griefs are!	
	Here they are but felt and seen with mischief's size,	
	But like to groves, being topp'd, they higher rise.	
CLEON	O Dionyza,	10
	Who wanteth food, and will not say he wants it,	
	Or can conceal his hunger till he famish?	
	Our tongues and sorrows do sound deep	
	Our woes into the air; our eyes do weep	

---

26. **He scap'd the land to perish on the seas:** Thaliard plans on telling Antiochus that Pericles drowned at sea. 35. **Commended to our master, not to us:** His absence is due to his own command, not our own.
SCENE IV.
0.*sd*. **Cleon.. Dionyza:** In Gower, they are named Stranguilio and Dionyse. 1. **rest:** forget our worries.
4. **That were to blow at fire in hope to quench it:** Roughly, that's like saying you'd like to start a fire to put one out. 9. **But like to groves, being topp'd, they higher rise:** Roughly, like trees that are trimmed, our sorrows continue to grow. 12. **till he famish:** until he is famished, starved. 13-15. **Our tongues and sorrows...proclaim them louder:** Both body and mind cry out in pain.

Till tongues fetch breath that may proclaim them louder;   15
That, if heaven slumber while their creatures want,
They may awake their helps to comfort them.
I'll then discourse our woes, felt several years,
And, wanting breath to speak, help me with tears.

DIONYZA   I'll do my best, sir.   20

CLEON   This Tharsus, o'er which I have the government,
A city on whom Plenty held full hand,
For Riches strew'd herself even in the streets;
Whose towers bore heads so high they kiss'd the clouds,
And strangers ne'er beheld but wond'red at;   25
Whose men and dames so jetted and adorn'd,
Like one another's glass to trim them by;
Their tables were stor'd full, to glad the sight,
And not so much to feed on as delight;
All poverty was scorn'd, and pride so great   30
The name of help grew odious to repeat.

DIONYZA   O, 'tis too true!

CLEON   But see what heaven can do! By this our change
Those mouths who, but of late, earth, sea, and air
Were all too little to content and please,   35
Although they gave their creatures in abundance,
As houses are defil'd for want of use,
They are now starv'd for want of exercise.
Those palates who, not yet two savours younger,
Must have inventions to delight the taste,   40
Would now be glad of bread, and beg for it.
Those mothers who to nuzzle up their babes
Thought naught too curious, are ready now
To eat those little darlings whom they lov'd.
So sharp are hunger's teeth that man and wife   45
Draw lots who first shall die to lengthen life.
Here stands a lord, and there a lady weeping;

---

16. **want:** their lack of food. 18. **felt several years:** The famine, presumably, has been, or feels like it has been, of long duration. 22. **Plenty:** Many modern editions do not capitalize, but this is probably in reference to Copia, goddess of plenty. 24. **heads:** the tops of the towers. 26. **jetted:** strutted proudly. 27. **glass:** mirror—ie. Everyone was so well dressed and pleased with their lot in life. Cleon may well be suggesting that the famine is a punishment for their arrogance. 35. **Were all too little to content and please:** Common pleasures were taken for granted. 39. **savours:** mouthfuls; sometimes emended to *summers*; in both cases the suggestion is that until recently, the citizens of Tarsus were spoiled by abundance. 40. **inventions:** exotic recipes. 42. **nuzzle:** nurture. 46. **Draw lots who first shall die to lengthen life:** Presumably so that the living can feed on the dead.

	Here many sink, yet those which see them fall	
	Have scarce strength left to give them burial.	
	Is not this true?	50
DIONYZA	Our cheeks and hollow eyes do witness it.	
CLEON	O, let those cities that of Plenty's cup	
	And her prosperities so largely taste	
	With their superfluous riots, hear these tears!	
	The misery of Tharsus may be theirs.	55

Enter a Lord.

LORD	Where's the Lord Governor?	
CLEON	Here.	
	Speak out thy sorrows which thou bring'st in haste,	
	For comfort is too far for us to expect.	
LORD	We have descried, upon our neighbouring shore,	60
	A portly sail of ships make hitherward.	
CLEON	I thought as much.	
	One sorrow never comes but brings an heir	
	That may succeed as his inheritor;	
	And so in ours, some neighbouring nation,	65
	Taking advantage of our misery,	
	Hath stuff'd these hollow vessels with their power,	
	To beat us down, the which are down already;	
	And make a conquest of unhappy me,	
	Whereas no glory's got to overcome.	70
LORD	That's the least fear; for, by the semblance	
	Of their white flags display'd, they bring us peace	
	And come to us as favorers, not as foes.	
CLEON	Thou speak'st like him's untutor'd to repeat:	
	Who makes the fairest show means most deceit.	75
	But bring they what they will and what they can,	
	What need we fear?	
	The ground's the lowest, and we are half-way there.	

---

48. **sink… fall:** decline in health and die. 49. **scarce:** barely enough. 51. **hollow eyes:** sign of starvation. 52. **Plenty's cup:** Copia's cup of abundance. See also 1.4.22. 54. **superfluous riots:** wasteful indulgence. 58-59. **Speak out thy sorrows which thou bring'st in haste,/ For comfort is too far for us to expect:** Roughly, what's the bad news? 61. **portly sail:** the wind-filled sail looks like a fat man's belly. Given that everyone in Tarsus is starving, the image foreshadows Pericles' offer of food and relief. 67. **stuff'd these hollow vessels with their power:** ships stuffed with soldiers. 71. **the least fear:** we need not fear invasion. 74. **Thou speak'st like him's untutor'd to repeat:** Roughly, You are being naive. 78. **The ground's the lowest, and we are half-way there:** on knees, defeated, near death.

	Go tell their general we attend him here,	
	To know for what he comes, and whence he comes,	80
	And what he craves.	

LORD   I go, my lord.   [*Exit.*]

CLEON   Welcome is peace, if he on peace consist;
          If wars, we are unable to resist.

Enter Pericles with Attendants.

PERICLES Lord Governor, for so we hear you are,   85
          Let not our ships and number of our men
          Be like a beacon fir'd t'amaze your eyes.
          We have heard your miseries as far as Tyre,
          And seen the desolation of your streets;
          Nor come we to add sorrow to your tears,   90
          But to relieve them of their heavy load;
          And these our ships you happily may think
          Are like the Troyan horse was stuff'd within
          With bloody veins, expecting overthrow,
          Are stor'd with corn to make your needy bread   95
          And give them life whom hunger starv'd half dead.

ALL   The gods of Greece protect you!
          And we'll pray for you.   [*They kneel.*]

PERICLES   Arise, I pray you, rise.
          We do not look for reverence, but for love,
          And harborage for ourself, our ships, and men.   100

CLEON   The which when any shall not gratify,
          Or pay you with unthankfulness in thought—
          Be it our wives, our children, or ourselves—
          The curse of heaven and men succeed their evils!
          Till when (the which, I hope, shall ne'er be seen) 105
          Your Grace is welcome to our town and us.

PERICLES Which welcome we'll accept, feast here awhile,
          Until our stars that frown lend us a smile.   *Exeunt.*

---

79. **Go tell their general:** their leader, in this case, Pericles. 83. **peace consist:** If his offer consists of peace. 87. **beacon fir'd:** Beacon fires were often used to signal invasion. 91. **heavy load:** Our loaded ships will relieve your heavy worries. 93. **Troyan horse was stuff'd within:** The Trojan horse, offered as a departing gift by the Greeks, was stuffed with soldiers who sacked Troy. 99. **We do not look for reverence, but for love:** Since Pericles does not mention that Antiochus is his deadly foe, the offer is not entirely altruistic. He is, in fact, bringing Tarsus into a potentially bloody conflict. This may account for Pericles' statement at 1.4.99, but if full disclosure is forthcoming, it is made offstage. 104. **succeed:** follow.

ACT II

Enter Gower.

GOWER   Here have you seen a mighty king
         His child iwis to incest bring;
         A better prince and benign lord,
         That will prove awful both in deed and word.
         Be quiet then, as men should be,   5
         Till he hath pass'd necessity.
         I'll show you those in troubles reign,
         Losing a mite, a mountain gain.
         The good in conversation,
         To whom I give my benison,   10
         Is still at Tharsus, where each man
         Thinks all is writ he speken can;
         And, to remember what he does,
         Build his statue to make him glorious.
         But tidings to the contrary   15
         Are brought your eyes. What need speak I?

*Dumb Show: Enter, at one door, Pericles, talking with Cleon; all the Train with them.
Enter, at another door, a Gentleman with a letter to Pericles. Pericles shows the letter to
Cleon. Pericles gives the Messenger a reward and knights him. Exit Pericles at one door
and Cleon at another, [with their Trains].*

         Good Helicane, that stay'd at home—
         Not to eat honey like a drone
         From others' labors, though he strive
         To killen bad, keep good alive,   20
         And to fulfil his prince' desire—
         Sends word of all that haps in Tyre:
         How Thaliard came full bent with sin
         And had intent to murder him;
         And that in Tharsus was not best   25

ACT II.
2. **iwis:** assuredly. 4. **That will prove awful both in deed and word:** A foreshadowing of Cleon's betrayal.
6. **pass'd necessity:** passed through extreme hardship. 8. **Losing a mite, a mountain gain:** Roughly, to be
rid of one small nuisance gains many more. 10. **benison:** blessing. 11-12. **where each man/Thinks all is
writ he speken can:** Roughly, where every man thinks all he speaks is holy writ, gospel; educated but with
false assurance. 14. **his statue to make him glorious:** a sign of false-idolatry. Cleon speaks like a holy man,
but his words are false as idols. 17.*sd.* **Dumb Show:** Silent show. A quaint dramaturgical device, akin to a
silent movie. —**Helicane:** Helicanus, Pericles' acting regent. 18. **Not to eat honey like a drone:** Roughly,
Helicanus is a worker bee, busy and productive. 20. **killen bad, keep good alive:** Roughly, attempts to
eradicate evil and sustain good. 23. **How Thaliard...to murder him:** As seen in 1.3.

Longer for him to make his rest.
He, doing so, put forth to seas,
Where when men been, there's seldom ease;
For now the wind begins to blow;
Thunder above, and deeps below,   30
Makes such unquiet that the ship
Should house him safe is wrack'd and split,
And he, good prince, having all lost,
By waves from coast to coast is tost.
All perishen of man, of pelf,   35
Ne aught escapen but himself;
Till fortune, tir'd with doing bad,
Threw him ashore, to give him glad.
And here he comes. What shall be next
Pardon old Gower; this longs the text.   [*Exit.*] 40

SCENE I. [*Pentapolis. An open place by the seaside.*]

Enter Pericles, wet.[†]

PERICLES   Yet cease your ire, you angry stars of heaven!
Wind, rain, and thunder, remember earthly man
Is but a substance that must yield to you;
And I, as fits my nature, do obey you.
Alas! the sea hath cast me on the rocks,   5

---

32. **Should house him safe is wrack'd and split:** Thaliard's lie that Pericles was drowned at sea very nearly comes true. 35-36. **All perishen of man, of pelf,/Ne aught escapen but himself:** Roughly, all men and goods are lost at sea; no one survives but Pericles. 40. **longs:** belongs to our story, which he, Gower, will not summarize.
SCENE I.
1-4. **Yet cease your ire, you angry stars of heaven!...do obey you:** Pericles' bad luck echoes George Wilkins' *Miseries of an Enforced Marriage* (1607): "Thus am I left like Sea-tost-Marriners,/My Fortunes being no more than my distresse,/Upon what shore soever I am driven,/ Be it good or bad, I must account it to heaven" (lines 1000-1003).

---

†   In David Thacker's 1990 RSC production, Nigel Terry grew into stature as he confronted his "Job-like fate" (Michael Schmidt, "Moral joy of Pericles." *The Daily Telegraph*, September 15, 1989). A similarly impressed Irving Wardle called him a "nautical Lear" ("The stuff of dreams." *The Times*, September 14, 1989). After Terry was injured, he was replaced by Rob Edwards, who was "personable, lively, clear-spoken," but far less heroic: "he suggests a rational Jane Austen hero on a singularly unpropitious tour of the Levant" (Michael Billington, "Pericles reborn." *The Guardian*, April 14, 1990). In the 2002 RSC production at the Roundhouse Theatre (dir. Adrian Noble), Ray Fearson's Pericles was "a dashing, virile hero," though one prone to "shouting too much" (Charles Spencer, "We should come to praise the RSC, not to bury them." *The Daily Telegraph*, July 8, 2002). In a 2003 production (Lyric Hammersmith), director Neil Bartlett had his Pericles (Will Keen) dressed as a pajamaed mental patient (Benedict Nightingale, "Pericles: the comeback." *The Times*, September 20, 2003).

Wash'd me from shore to shore, and left me breath
Nothing to think on but ensuing death.
Let it suffice the greatness of your powers
To have bereft a prince of all his fortunes,
And having thrown him from your wat'ry grave,   10
Here to have death in peace is all he'll crave.

Enter three Fishermen.‡

1. FISHERMAN   What ho, Pilch!

2. FISHERMAN   Ha, come and bring away the nets!

1. FISHERMAN   What, Patchbreech, I say!

3. FISHERMAN   What say you, master?   15

1. FISHERMAN   Look how thou stirr'st now! Come away, or I'll fetch thee with a wanion.

3. FISHERMAN   Faith, master, I am thinking of the poor men that were cast away before us even now.

1. FISHERMAN   Alas, poor souls! It grieved my heart to hear what pitiful cries they made to us to help them, when (well-a-day!) we could scarce help ourselves.   22

3. FISHERMAN   Nay, master, said not I as much when I saw the porpas, how he bounc'd and tumbled? They say they're half fish, half flesh. A plague on them! They ne'er come but I look to be wash'd. Master, I marvel how the fishes live in the sea.   26

1. FISHERMAN   Why, as men do aland—the great ones eat up the little ones. I can compare our rich misers to nothing so fitly as to a whale. 'A plays and tumbles, driving the poor fry before him, and at last devours them all at a mouthful. Such whales have I heard on o' th' land,

---

7. **Nothing to think on but ensuing death:** Reduced to a misery similar to that of Cleon, whom he relieved. 10. **wat'ry grave:** Tossed him out of the deadly sea. 11. **crave:** There is a sense here that Pericles longs for death, that his complaint is that he is still alive. Perhaps foreshadowing his depressive state in 5.1. 12.*sd.* **fishermen:** In Gower, Pericles, there named Appolinus, is rescued by one fisherman. —**Pilch:** to steal, here used as a nickname. 14. **Patchbreech:** A patch for, presumably, a shirt or sweater, full of holes, used here as a nickname. 16. **Look how thou stirr'st:** move it! 17. **wanion:** curse; ie— move it or I'll beat you with a vengeance. 18. **cast away:** Lost at sea during the recent storm. 23. **porpas:** porpoise; often associated with mermaids, thus half man-flesh, half-fish. 27. **the great ones eat up the little ones:** A powerful image of the predatory and merciless nature of the world, presently diluted by the fishermen's kindness.

---

‡   Director Adrian Jackson (RSC/Cardboard Citizens) transformed the fishermen into launderette attendants (Kate Bassett, "All washed up (on a shore of wet jumpers)." (*Independent on Sunday*, August 3, 2003).

who never leave gaping till they've swallow'd the whole parish—
church, steeple, bells, and all.   32

PERICLES   [*Aside.*] A pretty moral.

3. FISHERMAN   But, master, if I had been the sexton,
I would have been that day in the belfry.   35

2. FISHERMAN   Why, man?

3. FISHERMAN   Because he should have swallowed me too; and when I had been
in his belly, I would have kept such a jangling of the bells that he
should never have left till he cast bells, steeple, church, and parish
up again. But if the good King Simonides were of my mind—   40

PERICLES   [*Aside.*] Simonides?

3. FISHERMAN   He would purge the land of these drones that rob the bee of her
honey.

PERICLES   [*Aside.*] How from the finny subject of the sea
These fishers tell the infirmities of men,   45
And from their wat'ry empire recollect
All that may men approve or men detect!—
Peace be at your labor, honest fishermen.

2. FISHERMAN   Honest, good fellow? What's that? If it be a day fits you, scratch't
out of the calendar, and nobody look after it.   50

PERICLES   May see the sea hath cast upon your coast—

2. FISHERMAN   What a drunken knave was the sea to cast thee in our way!

PERICLES   A man whom both the waters and the wind,
In that vast tennis court, have made the ball
For them to play upon, entreats you pity him.   55
He asks of you that never us'd to beg.

1. FISHERMAN   No, friend? Cannot you beg? Here's them in our country of Greece
gets more with begging than we can do with working.

2. FISHERMAN   Canst thou catch any fishes then?

31-32. **they've swallow'd the whole parish—church, steeple, bells, and all:** If there is a clear theological
connection between fishermen and Christianity—an ancient symbol of Jesus is the fish—there may be a
possible echo here to Henry VIII, who appropriated/swallowed up all church lands—though describing
the Catholic church as a "little fish" is a stretch. 35. **belfry:** church tower. 37-38. **I had been in his belly:**
Another theological link?—Jonah in the belly of the whale. 40. **Simonides:** Named Artestrates in Gower;
his name is Altistrates in Twine. A further point: In Shakespeare, Simonides is a widower. His queen
lives in Gower's version. 42-43. **drones that rob the bee of her honey:** Identical to the description of the
hardworking and loyal Helicanus. See 2.18. 44. **finny:** fishy. 45. **fishers tell the infirmities of men:** Fish
as an allegory of man's sin and redemption. See 2.1.31-32, above. 51. **May:** You may. 52. **drunken knave
was the sea to cast thee in our way:** Drunk, soaked, vomited from the sea. 54. **tennis court:** Tennis, a
sport of kings.

PERICLES	I never practis'd it. 60
2. FISHERMAN	Nay, then thou wilt starve sure; for here's nothing to be got now-a-days unless thou canst fish for't.
PERICLES	What I have been I have forgot to know;
	But what I am, want teaches me to think on:
	A man throng'd up with cold; my veins are chill, 65
	And have no more of life than may suffice
	To give my tongue that heat to ask your help;
	Which if you shall refuse, when I am dead,
	For that I am a man, pray you see me buried.
1. FISHERMAN	Die koth-a? Now gods forbid't! And I have a gown here; come put it on; keep thee warm. Now, afore me, a handsome fellow! Come, thou shalt go home, and we'll have flesh for holidays, fish for fasting days, and moreo'er puddings and flapjacks; and thou shalt be welcome.
PERICLES	I thank you, sir. 75
2. FISHERMAN	Hark you, my friend. You said you could not beg?
PERICLES	I did but crave.
2. FISHERMAN	But crave? Then I'll turn craver too, and so I shall scape whipping.
PERICLES	Why, are all your beggars whipp'd then?
2. FISHERMAN	O, not all, my friend, not all! For if all your beggars were whipp'd, I would wish no better office than to be beadle. But, master, I'll go draw up the net. [Exit with Third Fisherman.]
PERICLES	[Aside.] How well this honest mirth becomes their labor!
1. FISHERMAN	Hark you, sir. Do you know where ye are?
PERICLES	Not well. 85
1. FISHERMAN	Why, I'll tell you. This is call'd Pentapolis, and our king the good Simonides.
PERICLES	The good Simonides do you call him?

---

62. **fish for't:** pun. Angling for a Court appointment. 63. **What I have been I have forgot to know:** Roughly, I am no longer a king; I am now a beggar relying upon your kindness. 64. **want:** poverty. 65. **throng'd:** numbed, overwhelmed. 67. **heat:** life, energy. 70. **koth-a?:** Quotha—so he quoted; so he said. 72-73. **flesh for holidays, fish for fasting days:** Roughly, you'll eat even when others go without. 78. **craver too, and so I shall scape whipping:** Begging was illegal, so, roughly: well, if calling yourself a "craver" works, then I'll call myself a craver too! 81. **beadle:** local constable, often meted out whipping for minor offenses. 83. **honest mirth becomes their labor:** Roughly, a simple life leads to simple, honest pleasure.

1. FISHERMAN	Ay, sir; and he deserves so to be call'd for his peaceable reign and good government. 90
PERICLES	He is a happy king, since he gains from his subjects the name of good by his government. How far is his court distant from this shore? 93
1. FISHERMAN	Marry, sir, half a day's journey. And I'll tell you, he hath a fair daughter, and tomorrow is her birthday, and there are princes and knights come from all parts of the world to joust and tourney for her love.
PERICLES	Were my fortunes equal to my desires, I could wish to make one there.
1. FISHERMAN	O, sir, things must be as they may; and what a man cannot get, he may lawfully deal for—his wife's soul. 101

Enter the two [other] Fishermen, drawing up a net.

2. FISHERMAN	Help, master, help! Here's a fish hangs in the net like a poor man's right in the law. 'Twill hardly come out. Ha! bots on't! 'tis come at last, and 'tis turn'd to a rusty armor.
PERICLES	An armor, friends? I pray you let me see it. 105
	Thanks, Fortune, yet, that, after all thy crosses,
	Thou givest me somewhat to repair myself!
	And though it was mine own, part of my heritage
	Which my dead father did bequeath to me,
	With this strict charge, even as he left his life, 110
	'Keep it, my Pericles. It hath been a shield
	'Twixt me and death'—and pointed to this brace;
	'For that it sav'd me, keep it. In like necessity—
	(The which the gods protect thee from!) may defend thee.'
	It kept where I kept, I so dearly lov'd it; 115
	Till the rough seas, that spare not any man,
	Took it in rage—though, calm'd, have given't again—
	I thank thee for't. My shipwrack now's no ill,
	Since I have here my father's gift in his will.
1. FISHERMAN	What mean you, sir? 120

---

96. **joust and tourney:** compete in chivalric games for her hand in marriage. 102-103. **Here's a fish hangs in the net like a poor man's right in the law:** Roughly, a man caught in the legal system is as powerless as a fish in a net. 106. **Fortune:** The goddess Fortuna, Lady Luck. 107. **repair myself:** repair my fortunes by winning the princess' hand in marriage. 108-11. **part of my heritage...Keep it:** Although Pericles has stated that he is willing to walk away from his aristocratic past, there seems to be a guiding force/fate that prompts him to join the tourney for Thaisa's hand in marriage. 118. **My shipwrack now's no ill:** My shipwreck is not so bad. Echoing George Wilkins' *The Miseries Of Enforced Marriage* (1607): "All hopes are shipwract, miserie comes on" (line 2214).

PERICLES	To beg of you, kind friends, this coat of worth,	
	For it was sometime target to a king.	
	I know it by this mark. He lov'd me dearly,	
	And for his sake I wish the having of it;	
	And that you'd guide me to your sovereign's court,	125
	Where with it I may appear a gentleman;	
	And if that ever my low fortune's better,	
	I'll pay your bounties; till then rest your debtor.	
1. FISHERMAN	Why, wilt thou tourney for the lady?	
PERICLES	I'll show the virtue I have borne in arms.	130
1. FISHERMAN	Why, do'ee take it, and the gods give thee good on't!	
2. FISHERMAN	Ay, but hark you, my friend! 'Twas we that made up this garment through the rough seams of the waters. There are certain condolements, certain vails. I hope, sir, if you thrive, you'll remember from whence you had it.	135
PERICLES	Believe't, I will.	
	By your furtherance I am cloth'd in steel;	
	And, spite of all the rupture of the sea,	
	This jewel holds his building on my arm.	
	Unto thy value I will mount myself	140
	Upon a courser whose delighted steps	
	Shall make the gazer joy to see him tread.	
	Only, my friend, I yet am unprovided	
	Of a pair of bases.	
2. FISHERMAN	We'll sure provide. Thou shalt have my best gown to make thee a pair; and I'll bring thee to the court myself.	146
PERICLES	Then honor be but a goal to my will, This day I'll rise, or else add ill to ill.	

[Exeunt.]

---

121. **this coat of worth:** iron coat, the armor that has washed ashore. 123. **mark:** The markings on the armor, though the crest of the shield will be changed to reflect his recent misfortunes. See 2.2.44. 126. **I may appear:** Of course, Pericles is far more than just a gentleman, but, given his reduced circumstances and his paranoia concerning Antiochus, his statement makes sense. 130. **virtue:** skill, but also harkening back to the chivalric notion that the virtuous cannot be defeated in single combat. 131. **do'ee:** do thee, do you. 133. **rough seams of the waters:** malapropism; he means the rough waters of the sea. 134. **certain condolements, certain vails:** He means doles (con*dole*ments); an allotment of money, food, etc.; vails, similarly, means *rewards*. 137. **I am cloth'd in steel:** armed in steel, perhaps also in friendship. 138. **rupture:** violence. 141. **courser:** horse. 144. **a pair of bases:** a skirt for the armor, formed of two shaped steel plates assembled side by side.

Scene II. [*Pentapolis. A public way or platform leading to the lists.*
A pavilion by the side of it for the reception of the King, Princess, Lords, &c.]

Enter [King] Simonides, with attendance, and Thaisa.

KING	Are the knights ready to begin the triumph?	
1. LORD	They are, my liege,	
	And stay your coming to present themselves.	
KING	Return them, we are ready; and our daughter,	
	In honor of whose birth these triumphs are,	5
	Sits here like beauty's child, whom nature gat	
	For men to see, and seeing wonder at. *[Exit a Lord.]*	
THAISA	It pleaseth you, my royal father, to express†	
	My commendations great, whose merit's less.	
KING	It's fit it should be so, for princes are	10
	A model which heaven makes like to itself.	
	As jewels lose their glory if neglected,	
	So princes their renowns if not respected.	
	'Tis now your honor, daughter, to entertain	
	The labor of each knight in his device.	15
THAISA	Which, to preserve mine honor, I'll perform.	

Scene II.

0.*sd. Thaisa:* In Gower, Thaisa has no name; in Twine's version, Thaisa is named Lucina. 1. **triumph:** combat. 4. **Return them:** Return them our greeting. 6-7. **whom nature gat/For men to see, and seeing wonder at:** Roughly, Nature made her for men to wonder at. 9. **My commendations great, whose merit's less:** Roughly, I'm not all that. 11. **A model which heaven makes like to itself:** Roughly, royals should be as virtuous as the heavens. 14. **to entertain:** read, decipher. 15. **knight in his device:** Each motto or emblem on the knights' shields.

---

† **The Doubling of Parts.** Minor actors in Shakespeare's company often doubled and tripled smaller parts. Many modern directors employ the same technique as a way to stress a recurrence of theme or an inversion of character. The doubling of Antiochus' daughter with Marina and Thasia is common, thereby underlying the repeated threat of incest. But other parts have been doubled as well. In a 1969 RSC production director Terry Hands cast Susan Fleetwood as Thaisa and Marina, Morgan Sheppard as both Antiochus and Boult, and Brenda Bruce as Dionyza and Bawd (Irving Wardle, "Parade of villainy and corruption." *The Times,* April 3, 1969). For director David Thacker's 1990 RSC production, Russell Dixon doubled as both Simonides and Boult (Michael Billington, "Pericles reborn." *The Guardian,* April 14, 1990). In director Phyllida Lloyd's 1994 production at the National Theatre, Kathryn Hunter played Antiochus, Cerimon, and the Bawd (Paul Taylor, "Under the weather." *The Independent,* May 24, 1994). Director James Roose-Evans (Ludlow Festival. Ludow Castle, 2000), cast Terence Knapp as Antiochus, Simonides, and Bawd (Paul Taylor, "Taboo or not taboo: that is the question." *The Independent,* June 28, 2000). In Neil Bartlett's 2003 Lyric Hammersmith production, Pascale Burgess played Marina and Antiochus' daughter, while Angela Down played Cerimon and the Bawd (Paul Taylor, "Pericles." *Independent Review,* October 3, 2003).

The First Knight passes by, [and his Squire shows his shield to the Princess].

KING   Who is the first that doth prefer himself?

THAISA   A knight of Sparta, my renowned father;
                    And the device he bears upon is shield
                    Is a black Ethiope reaching at the sun;   20
                    The word, "Lux tua vita mihi."

KING   He loves you well that holds his life of you.

                              The Second Knight.
                    Who is the second that presents himself?

THAISA   A prince of Macedon, my royal father;
                    And the device he bears upon his shield   25
                    Is an armed knight that's conquered by a lady;
                    The motto thus in Spanish, "Piu por dulzura que por fuerza."

                              Third Knight.

KING   And what's the third?

THAISA   The third of Antioch;
                    And his device, a wreath of chivalry;
                    The word, "Me pompae provexit apex."   30

                              Fourth Knight.

KING   What is the fourth?

THAISA   A burning torch that's turned upside down;
                    The word, "Quod me alit, me extinguit."

KING   Which shows that beauty hath his power and will,
                    Which can as well inflame as it can kill.   35

                              Fifth Knight.

THAISA   The fifth, an hand environed with clouds,
                    Holding out gold that's by the touchstone tried;
                    The motto thus, "Sic spectanda fides."

                              Sixth Knight [Pericles].

---

17. **doth prefer:** does present. 20. **Ethiope:** Ethiopian. 22. **He loves you well that holds his life of you:** The king translates. 24. **Macedon:** Famously, the birthplace of Alexander the Great. Why his shield is in as the Folger editors Mowat and Werstine describe it, "garbled Italian," is not explained. 27. **Piu por dulzura que por fuerza:** More by sweetness than by force. 28. **Antioch:** Why this knight does not recognize or, given Antiochus' known animosity, attack Pericles is not explained. Perhaps Pericles is in disguise, or unaccustomly wretched. 30. **Me pompae provexit apex:** The crown of glory is my motivation. 33. **Quod me alit, me extinguit:** Who feeds me, extinguishes me, or, roughly, challenge is what drives me. 38. **Sic spectanda fides:** Faith should be tested.

KING	And what's
	The sixth and last, the which the knight himself 40
	With such a graceful courtesy deliver'd?
THAISA	He seems to be a stranger; but his present is
	A withered branch that's only green at top;
	The motto, "In hac spe vivo."
KING	A pretty moral. 45
	From the dejected state wherein he is
	He hopes by you his fortunes yet may flourish.
1. LORD	He had need mean better than his outward show
	Can any way speak in his just commend;
	For by his rusty outside he appears 50
	To have practis'd more the whipstock than the lance.
2. LORD	He well may be a stranger, for he comes
	To an honor'd triumph strangely furnished.
3. LORD	And on set purpose let his armor rust
	Until this day, to scour it in the dust. 55
KING	Opinion's but a fool, that makes us scan
	The outward habit by the inward man.
	But stay, the knights are coming. We will withdraw
	Into the gallery. [*Exeunt.*]

Great shouts [within,] and all cry "The mean knight!"

---

43. **A withered branch that's only green at top:** thus rootless, a wanderer, or, perhaps, more hopefully, continuing the image found at 1.4.9.   44. **In hac spe vivo:** In this hope I live.   48. **He had need mean better than his outward show:** Roughly, he looks a bit rundown, down on his luck, poor. 51. **whipstock than the lance:** a horse whip, rather than a long wooden shaft. Roughly, he looks more like a cart driver than a knight at arms. 53-55. **an honor'd triumph strangely furnished...to scour it in the dust:** Without the proper attire. Turned into a joke. The sense is that they think he's a foreign yokel. 56-57. **Opinion's but a fool, that makes us scan/The outward habit by the inward man:** A sign of Simonides' discernment. 59. **the gallery:** In the playhouse, the balcony stage, on the second level of the tiring-house. 60. **The mean knight:** The poor-looking knight—ie. Pericles, who must have achieved some great victory.

SCENE III. [*Pentapolis. A hall of state; a banquet prepared.*]†

Enter the King [Simonides, Thaisa, Ladies, Lords,] and Knights, from tilting.

KING   Knights,
                To say you're welcome were superfluous.
                To place upon the volume of your deeds,
                As in a title-page, your worth in arms
                Were more than you expect, or more than's fit,   5
                Since every worth in show commends itself.
                Prepare for mirth, for mirth becomes a feast.
                You are princes and my guests.

THAISA   But you, my knight and guest;
                To whom this wreath of victory I give,   10
                And crown you king of this day's happiness.

PERICLES   'Tis more by Fortune, lady, than my merit.

KING   Call it by what you will, the day is yours;
                And here, I hope, is none that envies it.
                In framing an artist, art hath thus decreed,   15
                To make some good, but others to exceed;
                And you are her labor'd scholar. Come, queen o' th' feast,
                For, daughter, so you are; here take your place.
                Marshal the rest as they deserve their grace.

KNIGHTS   We are honor'd much by good Simonides.   20

KING   Your presence glads our days. Honor we love;
                For who hates honor hates the gods above.

MARSHAL   Sir, yonder is your place.

PERICLES   Some other is more fit.

SCENE III.
1. **superfluous:** unnecessary. 2-5. **volume of your deeds… you expect:** Addressed to all the knights. Roughly, if your deeds were a book, your actions today are but the table of contents inscribing your storied merits. 6. **commends itself:** speaks for itself. 7. **mirth:** a good time. 9. **But you:** suggests that Pericles seems oddly morose. See 2.3.54, below. 12. **Fortune:** Lady Luck. See 2.1.106. 15-16. **In framing an artist, art hath thus decreed,/ To make some good, but others to exceed:** Roughly, some are made better than others, and Nature has put a lot of work into you. 19. **as they deserve their grace:** as their graces (merits) deserve. 23. **Some other is more fit:** Someone more deserving, again, a sign of Pericles' modesty.

---

†   **The Tournament.** Shakespeare does not show the knights' tourney. In director Dominic Cooke's RSC production (2006), the tournament is spoofed with a mock steeplechase and a parody of Olympic swimming (Benedict Nightingale, "*The Winter's Tale/Pericles.*" *The Times*, November 17, 2006).

The knights' tourney, missing from the play, often added by directors. *Pericles*, 1969, directed by Terry Hands, designed by Timothy O'Brien. Jousting in the court of Simonides. The cast, from left to right is, Knight (David Bailey), Simonides (Derek Smith), Gower (Emrys James), Thaisa (Susan Fleetwood), Knight (Boyd MacKenzie). (Reg Wilson © Royal Shakespeare Company)

1. KNIGHT	Contend not, sir; for we are gentlemen	
	That neither in our hearts nor outward eyes	25
	Envy the great nor shall the low despise.	
PERICLES	You are right courteous knights.	
KING	Sit, sir, sit.	
THAISA	[*Aside.*] By Jove, I wonder, that is king of thoughts,	
	These cates resist me, he not thought upon.	
	By Juno, that is queen of marriage,	30
	All viands that I eat do seem unsavoury,	
	Wishing him my meat.— [*To her father.*] Sure he's a gallant gentleman.	
KING	He's but a country gentleman.	
	Has done no more than other knights have done;	
	Has broken a staff or so; so let it pass.	35

26. **Envy the great nor shall the low despise:** Pericles is both, great in arms but poor in appearance. 29. **cates...not thought upon:** Difficult. Perhaps, I can't think of delicacies (*cates*) when I see him, Pericles. Though the lines are in some editions ascribed to the King, they clearly work better coming from Thaisa. 30. **Juno, that is queen of marriage:** Zeus' wife and his sister. Perhaps a link to incest is here implied? See performance note at 5.1.103, below, and HOW TO READ *PERICLES, PRINCE OF TYRE* AS PERFORMANCE. 33. **country:** poor, provincial. 35. **let it pass:** forget about him.

THAISA	To me he seems like diamond to glass.

PERICLES   [*Aside.*] Yon king's to me like to my father's picture,
Which tells me in that glory once he was;
Had princes sit like stars about his throne,
And he the sun for them to reverence;   40
None that beheld him but, like lesser lights,
Did vail their crowns to his supremacy;
Where now his son's like a glowworm in the night,
The which hath fire in darkness, none in light.
Whereby I see that Time's the king of men;   45
He's both their parent, and he is their grave,
And gives them what he will, not what they crave.

KING   What, are you merry, knights?

KNIGHTS   Who can be other in this royal presence?

KING   Here, with a cup that's stor'd unto the brim—   50
As you do love, fill to your mistress' lips—
We drink this health to you.

KNIGHTS   We thank your Grace.

KING   Yet pause awhile.
Yon knight doth sit too melancholy,
As if the entertainment in our court   55
Had not a show might countervail his worth.
Note it not you, Thaisa?

THAISA   What is't to me, my father?

KING   O, attend, my daughter.
Princes, in this, should live like gods above,   60
Who freely give to every one that comes
To honor them;
And princes not doing so are like to gnats,
Which make a sound, but kill'd are wond'red at.
Therefore to make his entertain more sweet,   65
Here, say we drink this standing bowl of wine to him.

---

36. **he seems like diamond to glass:** All the rest seem inferior compared to him. 39-40. **princes sit like stars...And he the sun for them to reverence:** He sat like a god among men. 42. **vail:** lower. 43. **Where now his son's like a glowworm in the night:** Compared to the luminous power of his father, Pericles is a glowworm, a speck seen in the darkness. 45. **Whereby I see that Time's the king of men:** Even kings grow old and die. 50. **stor'd:** filled. 51. **fill:** drink to, toast. 54. **Yon knight doth sit too melancholy:** Pericles seems sad and alone. 56. **countervail his worth:** worthy of him. 57. **Note it not you:** Have you noticed. 60. **should live like gods above:** Presumably with honor, though the Greco-Roman pantheon has few examples of principled behavior. 63. **gnats:** bugs, unnoticed, unless as irritants. 66. **standing bowl:** a bowl with legs, here probably a ceremonial cup of some kind.

THAISA	Alas, my father, it befits not me
	Unto a stranger knight to be so bold!
	He may my proffer take for an offence,
	Since men take women's gifts for impudence. 70
KING	How?
	Do as I bid you, or you'll move me else.
THAISA	[*Aside.*] Now, by the gods, he could not please me better.
KING	And furthermore tell him we desire to know of him
	Of whence he is, his name and parentage. 75
THAISA	The King my father, sir, has drunk to you—
PERICLES	I thank him.
THAISA	Wishing it so much blood unto your life.
PERICLES	I thank both him and you, and pledge him freely.
THAISA	And further, he desires to know of you 80
	Of whence you are, your name and parentage.
PERICLES	A gentleman of Tyre; my name, Pericles;
	My education been in arts and arms;
	Who, looking for adventures in the world,
	Was by the rough seas reft of ships and men 85
	And, after shipwreck, driven upon this shore.
THAISA	[*To her father.*] He thanks your Grace; names himself Pericles,
	A gentleman of Tyre,
	Who only by misfortune of the seas
	Bereft of ships and men, cast on this shore. 90
KING	Now, by the gods, I pity his misfortune
	And will awake him from his melancholy.
	Come, gentlemen, we sit too long on trifles
	And waste the time which looks for other revels.
	Even in your armors, as you are address'd, 95
	Will very well become a soldier's dance.
	I will not have excuse, with saying this
	Loud music is too harsh for ladies' heads,

---

69. **proffer take for an offence:** He might think me too forward, immodest. 72. **move:** anger. 76. **drunk to you:** toasted the room in your honor. 78. **Wishing it so much blood unto your life:** Roughly, wishing you a long and a good life. 79. **pledge him:** Drink to his health, acknowledge the honor he bestows. 81. **whence you are:** where you come from. 85. **reft:** bereft. 92. **awake him from his melancholy:** cheer him up. 94. **revels:** entertainments. 95. **address'd:** dressed, though it is hard to see how they might dance in full armor.

Since they love men in arms as well as beds.   *They dance.*[†]

So, this was well ask'd, 'twas so well perform'd.   100

[*To Pericles.*] Come, sir.

Here is a lady that wants breathing too;

And I have heard, you knights of Tyre

Are excellent in making ladies trip,

And that their measures are as excellent.   105

PERICLES   In those that practice them they are, my lord.

KING   O, that's as much as you would be denied

Of your fair courtesy.   [*The Knights and Ladies*] *dance.*

Unclasp, unclasp!

Thanks, gentlemen, to all; all have done well,

[*To Pericles*] But you the best.—Pages and lights, to conduct   110

These knights unto their several lodgings!—Yours, sir,

We have given order to be next our own.

PERICLES   I am at your Grace's pleasure.

KING   Princes, it is too late to talk of love;

And that's the mark I know you level at.   115

Therefore each one betake him to his rest;

Tomorrow all for speeding do their best.   [*Exeunt.*]

SCENE IV. [*Tyre. The house of Helicanus, the Governor.*]

Enter Helicanus and Escanes.

HELICANUS   No, Escanes; know this of me—

Antiochus from incest liv'd not free;

---

99. **Since they love men in arms as well as beds:** Considering the only woman present seems to be his daughter, the line is grossly inappropriate. 102. **breathing:** wants exercise, excitement, possibly enticement. 104. **trip:** dance, with bawdy pun—trip up, fall down together in each other's arms. 105. **measures:** dances, punning on seduction?—smooth moves. 108. **Unclasp, unclasp:** Presumably, Pericles and Thaisa are dancing closely. 110-111. **Pages and lights, to conduct...unto their several lodgings:** Pages with lanterns will conduct you to your rooms. 114. **to talk of love:** to romance Thaisa. 115. **the mark I know you level at:** Why you are all here. 117. **speeding do their best:** succeed in doing their best.

† **The Use of Song, Dance and Costume.** The 1984 BBC TV version included a ritual sword dance, one in which Pericles (Mike Gwilym) did not participate; but he thereafter join Thaisa (Juliet Stevenson) for a Neo-Elizabethan country dance. In director Phyllida Lloyd's 1994 production at the National Theatre, critic Paul Taylor complained of the cluttered used of "devices and gimmicks" (Paul Taylor, "Under the weather." *The Independent*, May 24, 1994); John Gross could make no sense of the costumed variety ("All singing, all dancing, no feeling." *Sunday Telegraph*, May 22, 1994); Charles Spencer complained that Lloyd seemed determined to turn the play into "an avant-garde pantomime" ("Shakespeare in silly hats," *Daily Telegraph*, May 23, 1994).

	For which, the most high gods not minding longer	
	To withhold the vengeance that they had in store,	
	Due to this heinous capital offence,	5
	Even in the height and pride of all his glory,	
	When he was seated in a chariot	
	Of an inestimable value, and his daughter with him,	
	A fire from heaven came and shrivell'd up	
	Their bodies, even to loathing; for they so stunk	10
	That all those eyes ador'd them ere their fall	
	Scorn now their hand should give them burial.	

ESCANES   'Twas very strange.

HELICANUS   And yet but justice; for though
            This king were great, his greatness was no guard   15
            To bar heaven's shaft, but sin had his reward.

ESCANES   'Tis very true.

Enter two or three Lords.

1. LORD   See, not a man in private conference
            Or council has respect with him but he.

2. LORD   It shall no longer grieve without reproof.   20

3. LORD   And curs'd be he that will not second it!

1. LORD   Follow me then. Lord Helicane, a word.

HELICANUS   With me? and welcome. Happy day, my lords.

1. LORD   Know that our griefs are risen to the top
            And now at length they overflow their banks.   25

HELICANUS   Your griefs? for what? Wrong not your prince you love.

1. LORD   Wrong not yourself then, noble Helicane;
            But if the prince do live, let us salute him,
            Or know what ground's made happy by his breath.
            If in the world he live, we'll seek him out;   30
            If in his grave he rest, we'll find him there
            And be resolv'd he lives to govern us,

SCENE IV.
4. **that they had in store:** that they had coming. 9. **fire from heaven came:** Signaling a Judeo-Christian deity by echoing 2Kings 1:14: "Behold, there came fire down from heaven" (Geneva Bible version). 15. **This king were great, his greatness was no guard:** Echoing Simonides' proverb at 2.3.60. 19. **respect with him but he:** Obscure. Perhaps, no one but Escanes can meet privately with Helicanus. A signs of the Lords' squabbling nature? 20. **It shall no longer grieve without reproof:** Roughly, we will no longer suffer in silence. 24-25. **Know that our griefs are risen to the top/ And now at length they overflow their banks:** Roughly, our unhappiness is like a flooding river; we can't hold it back anymore. 29. **what ground's:** what ground he walks on, if, in fact he is still alive. 32. **he lives:** if he lives.

| | Or, dead, give 's cause to mourn his funeral, |
| | And leave us to our free election. |

2. LORD	Whose death's indeed the strongest in our censure;	35
	And knowing this kingdom, if without a head,
	Like goodly buildings left without a roof,
	Soon fall to ruin, your noble self,
	That best know how to rule and how to reign,
	We thus submit unto—our sovereign.	40

| ALL | Live, noble Helicane! |

HELICANUS	For honor's cause forbear your suffrages.
	If that you love Prince Pericles, forbear.
	Take I your wish, I leap into the seas,
	Where's hourly trouble for a minute's ease.	45
	A twelvemonth longer let me entreat you
	To forbear the absence of your king;
	If in which time expir'd he not return,
	I shall with aged patience bear your yoke.
	But if I cannot win you to this love,	50
	Go search like nobles, like noble subjects,
	And in your search spend your adventurous worth;
	Whom if you find and win unto return,
	You shall like diamonds sit about his crown.

1. LORD	To wisdom he's a fool that will not yield;	55
	And since Lord Helicane enjoineth us,
	We with our travels will endeavour it.

| HELICANUS | Then you love us, we you, and we'll clasp hands. |
| | When peers thus knit, a kingdom ever stands.   *Exeunt.* |

---

34. **free election:** to choose a new ruler—ie. Helicanus. 35. **death's indeed the strongest in our censure:** It's more likely, in our opinion, that he is dead. 36-37. **And knowing this kingdom, if without a head,/Like goodly buildings left without a roof:** Roughly, a kingdom without a king is like a room without a roof. 42. **forbear:** refrain. 42. **suffrages:** your vote, support. 44. **I leap into the seas:** flee as Pericles did. 49. **bear your yoke:** suffer to do as you ask, become your slave/king. 50. **this love:** this agreement. 52. **your adventurous worth:** Sending these knights in quest of Pericles echoes the Arthurian romances, in which knights search for the Holy Grail. Such adventures in *Pericles* are common. Note the many knights who try their luck at Antiochus' and Simonides' respective Courts. 54. **diamonds sit about his crown:** Roughly, if you convince Pericles to return, your continued loyalty will enhance his power, his crown. 57. **We with our travels will endeavour it:** We never see any of these quasi-quest-knights in their travels, though it is referred to again by Gower in Act 3. This may indicate some abridgement. 58. **Then you love us:** You have proven your love/loyalty. 59. **When peers thus knit, a kingdom ever stands:** Roughly, when we stand as one, we are invincible.

SCENE V. [*Pentapolis. The Palace of King Simonides.*]

Enter the King [Simonides], reading of a letter at one door. The Knights meet him.

1. KNIGHT	Good morrow to the good Simonides.
KING	Knights, from my daughter this I let you know,
	That for this twelvemonth she'll not undertake
	A married life.
	Her reason to herself is only known,

5

	Which from her by no means can I get.
2. KNIGHT	May we not get access to her, my lord?
KING	Faith, by no means. She hath so strictly tied her
	To her chamber that it is impossible.
	One twelve moons more she'll wear Diana's livery.

10

This by the eye of Cynthia hath she vow'd,
And on her virgin honor will not break it.

2. KNIGHT   Loath to bid farewell, we take our leaves.   *Exeunt [Knights].*

KING   So,
They are well dispatch'd. Now to my daughter's letter.
She tells me here, she'll wed the stranger knight,   15
Or never more to view nor day nor light.
'Tis well, mistress; your choice agrees with mine;
I like that well. Nay, how absolute she's in't,
Not minding whether I dislike or no!
Well, I do commend her choice;   20
And will no longer have it be delay'd.
Soft! here he comes; I must dissemble it.

Enter Pericles.

PERICLES   All fortune to the good Simonides!

KING   To you as much, sir! I am beholding to you
For your sweet music this last night. I do   25
Protest my ears were never better fed
With such delightful pleasing harmony.

SCENE V.
1. **morrow:** day. 3. **twelvemonth:** one full year. 7. **get access to her:** speak to her. 8-9. **tied her/ To her chamber:** kept to her room. 10. **Diana's:** goddess of chastity. 11. **Cynthia:** goddess of the moon, often associated with Diana. 14. **dispatch'd:** rid of, sent away. 18. **absolute:** inflexible. 22. **I must dissemble it:** Pretend I think that I am unhappy that my daughter is in love with Pericles. 25. **For your sweet music this last night:** The text offers no such scene. This may indicate some abridgement. For more on this missing song, see HOW TO READ *PERICLES, PRINCE OF TYRE* AS PERFORMANCE.

PERICLES	It is your Grace's pleasure to commend; Not my desert.	
KING	Sir, you are music's master.	
PERICLES	The worst of all her scholars, my good lord.	30
KING	Let me ask you one thing: what do you think Of my daughter, sir?	
PERICLES	A most virtuous princess.	
KING	And she is fair too, is she not?	
PERICLES	As a fair day in summer—wondrous fair.	
KING	Sir, my daughter thinks very well of you; Ay, so well that you must be her master And she will be your scholar. Therefore look to it.	35
PERICLES	I am unworthy for her schoolmaster.	
KING	She thinks not so. Peruse this writing else.	
PERICLES	[*Aside.*] What's here? A letter, that she loves the knight of Tyre? 'Tis the King's subtlety to have my life.— O, seek not to entrap me, gracious lord, A stranger and distressed gentleman, That never aim'd so high to love your daughter, But bent all offices to honor her.	40 45
KING	Thou hast bewitch'd my daughter, and thou art A villain.	
PERICLES	By the gods, I have not! Never did thought of mine levy offence; Nor never did my actions yet commence A deed might gain her love or your displeasure.	 50
KING	Traitor, thou liest!	
PERICLES	Traitor?	
KING	Ay, traitor.	

29. **Sir, you are music's master:** In Gower's version Pericles is schoolmaster to the princess. 38. **for her:** to be her. 42. **'Tis the King's subtlety to have my life:** An excuse to have me killed. 45. **never aim'd so high to love your daughter:** An odd statement, since he came to court in his motley armor to win her hand. 46. **all offices:** all his efforts. 47. **hast bewitch'd:** used witchcraft. 49. **levy offence:** to make war, to offend. 51. **A deed might gain her love or your displeasure:** Again, it's hard to understand how this can be true.

PERICLES	Even in his throat—unless it be the King— That calls me traitor, I return the lie.
KING	[*Aside.*] Now, by the gods, I do applaud his courage.

55

PERICLES	My actions are as noble as my thoughts, That never relish'd of a base descent. I came unto your court for honor's cause, And not to be a rebel to her state; And he that otherwise accounts of me, This sword shall prove he's honor's enemy.

60

KING	No? Here comes my daughter, she can witness it.

Enter Thaisa.

PERICLES	Then, as you are as virtuous as fair, Resolve your angry father if my tongue Did e'er solicit, or my hand subscribe To any syllable that made love to you.

65

THAISA	Why, sir, say if you had, Who takes offence at that would make me glad?

KING	Yea, mistress, are you so peremptory? [*Aside.*] I am glad on't with all my heart.— I'll tame you; I'll bring you in subjection! Will you, not having my consent, Bestow your love and your affections Upon a stranger?— [*Aside.*] who, for aught I know, May be (nor can I think the contrary) As great in blood as I myself.— Therefore hear you, mistress: either frame Your will to mine—and you, sir, hear you, Either be rul'd by me, or I'll make you— Man and wife. Nay, come, your hands and lips must seal it too;

70

75

80

53-54. **Even in his throat...I return the lie:** Echoing George Wilkins' *The Miseries Of Enforced Marriage* (1607): "And I tell thee (setting thy worth, knighthood aside) he lyes in his throat that saies so" (lines 1621-1622). 57. **never relish'd:** relish, taste, savory, here suggesting a hunger for. Echoing George Wilkins' *The Miseries Of Enforced Marriage* (1607): "A relish of thy sorrow and misfortune" (line 2377). 59. **rebel to her state:** Would never attack, undermine honor. 66-67. **Did e'er solicit, or my hand subscribe/To any syllable that made love to you:** Roughly, whether I ever tried to flirt with you or seduce you. 70. **peremptory:** determined. 73. **not having my consent:** my permission, my blessing. 78. **frame:** bend, remake. 81. **Man and wife:** Clearly delivered for comic effect. He threats and berates only to give them what they both desire.

	And being join'd, I'll thus your hopes destroy,	
	And for a further grief—God give you joy!	
	What, are you both pleas'd?	
THAISA	Yes, if you love me, sir?	85
PERICLES	Even as my life my blood that fosters it!	
KING	What, are you both agreed?	
BOTH	Yes, if't please your Majesty.	
KING	It pleaseth me so well that I will see you wed;	
	And then, with what haste you can, get you to bed. *Exeunt.*	90

ACT III

Enter Gower.

GOWER   Now sleep yslacked hath the rout;
No din but snores the house about,
Made louder by the o'erfed breast
Of this most pompous marriage feast.
The cat, with eyne of burning coal,   5
Now couches fore the mouse's hole;
And crickets sing at the oven's mouth,
E'er the blither for their drouth.
Hymen hath brought the bride to bed,
Where, by the loss of maidenhead,   10
A babe is moulded. Be attent,
And time that is so briefly spent
With your fine fancies quaintly eche.
What's dumb in show I'll plain with speech.

Dumb Show. Enter Pericles and Simonides at one door, with Attendants; a Messenger meets them, kneels, and gives Pericles a letter. Pericles shows it Simonides. The Lords kneel to him, [Pericles]. Then enter Thaisa with child, with Lychorida, a nurse. The

---

83-84. **I'll thus your hopes destroy,/And for a further grief:** Comic, destroy hope by making their dreams come true. 90. **with what haste you can, get you to bed:** Comic, though inappropriate considering this is coming from Thaisa's father.
ACT III.
1. **yslacked hath the rout:** slacked the crowd, ie—they are inactive. 2. **din:** sound. 3. **o'erfed:** overfed. 5. **eyne:** eye. 8. **blither for their drouth:** Roughly, chirp to keep dry. 9. **Hymen:** God of marriage. 11. **moulded:** conceived. 13. **eche:** eke, gain with difficulty, eke out. 14. **dumb in show:** See 2.16.*sd*. 14.*sd*. **Lychorida:** Her name is Ligozides in Twine's version.

King shows her the letter; she rejoices. She and Pericles take leave of her father, and depart [with Lychorida and their Attendants. Then exeunt Simonides and the rest].

By many a dern and painful perch   15
Of Pericles the careful search,
By the four opposing coigns
Which the world together joins,
Is made with all due diligence
That horse and sail and high expense   20
Can stead the quest. At last from Tyre,
Fame answering the most strange enquire,
To th' court of King Simonides
Are letters brought, the tenor these:
Antiochus and his daughter dead,   25
The men of Tyrus on the head
Of Helicanus would set on
The crown of Tyre, but he will none.
The mutiny he there hastes t' oppress;
Says to 'em, if King Pericles   30
Come not home in twice six moons,
He, obedient to their dooms,
Will take the crown. The sum of this,
Brought hither to Pentapolis,
Y-ravished the regions round,   35
And every one with claps can sound,
"Our heir apparent is a king!
Who dreamt, who thought of such a thing?"
Brief, he must hence depart to Tyre.
His queen with child makes her desire   40
(Which who shall cross?) along to go.
Omit we all their dole and woe.
Lychorida her nurse she takes,
And so to sea. Their vessel shakes
On Neptune's billow; half the flood   45
Hath their keel cut: but Fortune's mood

---

15. **many a dern and painful perch:** Roughly, many a dangerous and laborious search. 17. **coigns:** corners, the four corners of the earth. 19. **all due diligence:** The search for Pericles; see 2.4.57, above. 26. **Tyrus:** Pericles' capital city, in modern-day Lebanon, mentioned in Ezekiel 26: 3: "Therefore thus saith the Lord GOD; Behold, I am against thee, O Tyrus, and will cause many nations to come up against thee, as the sea causeth his waves to come up" (Geneva Bible version). 28. **he will none:** Helicanus refused to be crowned. 33. **Will take the crown:** As explained in 2.4. 35. **Y-ravished:** ravished or enraptured. 37. **Our heir apparent is a king:** Simonides' heir, Pericles, is a ruler in his own right, much to the surprise of the people of Pentapolis. 40. **with child:** pregnant. 40. **her desire:** Her desire to join him. 42. **dole:** grief. 45. **Neptune's:** God of the sea. 46. **keel:** part of a ship's hull or bottom.

Varies again; the grisled North
Disgorges such a tempest forth
That, as a duck for life that dives,
So up and down the poor ship drives.   50
The lady shrieks, and, well-a-near,
Does fall in travail with her fear;
And what ensues in this fell storm
Shall for itself itself perform.
I nill relate, action may   55
Conveniently the rest convey,
Which might not what by me is told.
In your imagination hold
This stage the ship, upon whose deck
The sea-tost Pericles appears to speak.   *Exit.*   60

SCENE I.†

Enter Pericles a-shipboard.

PERICLES   Thou god of this great vast, rebuke these surges,
Which wash both heaven and hell; and thou that hast
Upon the winds command, bind them in brass,
Having recall'd them from the deep! O, still
Thy deaf'ning dreadful thunders; gently quench   5
Thy nimble sulphurous flashes!—O, how, Lychorida,
How does my queen?—Thou stormest venomously;
Wilt thou spet all thyself? The seaman's whistle
Is as a whisper in the ears of death,

47-48. **grisled North... Disgorges:** There is some confusion here. The god of the north wind was Boreas, whose chilling frost might account for the grizzled (ie. icicled) descriptive. As for "Disgorges"—here used in references to the sea—that activity was the purview of Charybdis, who thrice daily swallowed the sea, and thrice threw it up again. 52. **travail:** pain, here of childbirth. 55. **I nill relate:** I will not relate but show. 58. **In your imagination hold:** Roughly, use your imagination.
SCENE I.
1. **vast:** vast sea.—**rebuke these surges:** Echoing Psalms 69: "Let not the water flood drowne mee... Rebuke hath broken mine heart, and I am full of heavinesse, and I looked for some to have pitie on me, but there was none: and for comforters, but I found none" (Geneva Bible version). 3. **bind them in brass:** A reference to the god Aeolus, who keeps the wind in a brass cave. 4. **still:** calm. 6. **sulphurous flashes:** lightning from the storm. 7. **stormest venomously:** the wind and rain seems to spit poison, harken death. 8. **spet:** spit.

---

†   **The Storm.** The 1984 BBC TV production had a full-sized boat tossing on what was clearly a soundstage. David Thacker's 1989, RSC's production, rather than employing hydraulics or projecting images of stormy seas, simply had actors sway back and forth.

Unheard.—Lychorida!—Lucina, O   10
Divinest patroness and midwife gentle
To those that cry by night, convey thy deity
Aboard our dancing boat; make swift the pangs
Of my queen's travails!

Enter Lychorida [with an Infant].

Now, Lychorida!

LYCHORIDA   Here is a thing too young for such a place,   15
Who, if it had conceit, would die, as I
Am like to do. Take in your arms this piece
Of your dead queen.

PERICLES   How? how, Lychorida?

LYCHORIDA   Patience, good sir; do not assist the storm.
Here's all that is left living of your queen—   20
A little daughter. For the sake of it,
Be manly and take comfort.

PERICLES   .   O you gods!
Why do you make us love your goodly gifts
And snatch them straight away? We here below
Recall not what we give, and therein may   25
Vie honor with you.

LYCHORIDA   Patience, good sir,
Even for this charge.

PERICLES   Now mild may be thy life!
For a more blusterous birth had never babe;
Quiet and gentle thy conditions! for
Thou art the rudeliest welcome to this world   30
That ever was prince's child. Happy what follows!
Thou hast as chiding a nativity
As fire, air, water, earth, and heaven can make,
To herald thee from the womb. Even at the first
Thy loss is more than can thy portage quit   35

---

10. **Lucina:** or, in the Greek, Eileithyia, goddess of childbirth. 14. **Now:** How now, or What is the news? 16. **conceit:** understanding. 17-18. **this piece/ Of your dead queen:** The babe is made in part from her mother, thus a piece of her. 22. **manly:** do not cry, mourn her loss. 24-26. **We here below... Vie honor with you:** Roughly, the gods greedily take back all they give; man does not. Therefore, man may be said to be more generous and, thus, in that one regard, superior to the gods. 27. **this charge:** this burden—ie. the care of the child. 29. **thy conditions:** circumstances, condition in life. 30. **rudeliest:** rudest, roughest. 31. **Happy what follows:** Roughly, after this unlucky beginning, your life will be all smooth sailing. 32. **nativity:** birth with reference to place or attendant circumstances—thus her name, Marina, born at sea. 33-34. **As fire, air, water, earth... from the womb:** All the elements seemed to clash at your birth. 35. **Thy portage:** Obscure. Perhaps, your burden.

With all thou canst find here. Now the good gods
Throw their best eyes upon't!

Enter two Sailors.

1. SAILOR	What courage, sir? God save you!
PERICLES	Courage enough. I do not fear the flaw;

It hath done to me the worst. Yet for the love   40
Of this poor infant, this fresh new seafarer,
I would it would be quiet.

1. SAILOR   Slack the bolins there! Thou wilt not, wilt thou? Blow, and split
thyself.   44

2. SAILOR   But searoom, an the brine and cloudy billow kiss the moon, I care
not.

1. SAILOR   Sir, your queen must overboard. The sea works high, the wind is
loud, and will not lie till the ship be clear'd of the dead.

PERICLES   That's your superstition.   49

1. SAILOR   Pardon us, sir. With us at sea it hath been still observed, and we are
strong in custom. Therefore briefly yield 'er; for she must overboard
straight.

PERICLES   As you think meet. Most wretched queen!

LYCHORIDA   Here she lies, sir.

PERICLES   A terrible childbed hast thou had, my dear;   55
No light, no fire. Th' unfriendly elements
Forgot thee utterly; nor have I time
To give thee hallow'd to thy grave, but straight
Must cast thee, scarcely coffin'd, in the ooze;
Where, for a monument upon thy bones,   60
And e'er-remaining lamps, the belching whale
And humming water must o'erwhelm thy corpse
Lying with simple shells. O Lychorida,
Bid Nestor bring me spices, ink and paper,
My casket and my jewels; and bid Nicander   65
Bring me the satin coffer. Lay the babe

---

39. **flaw:** windflaw, a sudden, usually brief windstorm or gust of wind. 40. **It hath done to me the worst:** Roughly, the storm has done it's worst; what have I now to fear? 43. **bolins:** bowlines, rope attached to the weather leech of a square sail. 45. **an the brine and cloudy billow kiss the moon:** Roughly, if the seas kissed the skies. 48. **clear'd of the dead:** The sailors think that a dead body on board is a curse. 52. **straight:** right away. 55. **childbed:** The circumstance or situation of a woman giving birth to a child. 59. **the ooze:** sandy bottom of the sea.

	Upon the pillow. Hie thee, whiles I say A priestly farewell to her. Suddenly, woman. [*Exit Lychorida.*]	
2. Sailor	Sir, we have a chest beneath the hatches, caulk'd and bitumed ready.	
Pericles	I thank thee. Mariner, say, what coast is this?	70
2. Sailor	We are near Tharsus.	
Pericles	Thither, gentle mariner, Alter thy course for Tyre. When canst thou reach it?	
2. Sailor	By break of day, if the wind cease.	
Pericles	O, make for Tharsus! There will I visit Cleon, for the babe Cannot hold out to Tyrus. There I'll leave it At careful nursing. Go thy ways, good mariner; I'll bring the body presently. *Exeunt.*	75

SCENE II. [*Ephesus. Cerimon's house*].

Enter Lord Cerimon, with a Servant [and some Persons who have been shipwrecked].

Cerimon	Philemon, ho!	

Enter Philemon.

Philemon	Doth my lord call?	
Cerimon	Get fire and meat for these poor men. 'T 'as been a turbulent and stormy night.	
Servant	I have been in many; but such a night as this Till now I ne'er endured.	5
Cerimon	Your master will be dead ere you return. There's nothing can be minist'red to nature That can recover him. [*To Philemon*] Give this to the pothecary, And tell me how it works. [*Exeunt all but Cerimon.*]	10

Enter two Gentlemen.

1. Gentleman	Good morrow.
2. Gentleman	Good morrow to your lordship.
Cerimon	Gentlemen, why do you stir so early?

---

68. **Suddenly:** quickly. 69. **caulk'd and bitumed ready:** watertight. 77. **hold out to:** hold out until, i.e. the baby will die without proper care.
Scene II.
4. **turbulent:** rough. 7. **master will be dead ere you return:** Cerimon has both scientific and perhaps even mystic powers. 9. **pothecary:** apothecary, pharmacist.

1. GENTLEMAN   Sir,
          Our lodgings, standing bleak upon the sea,
          Shook as the earth did quake.   15
          The very principals did seem to rend,
          And all to topple. Pure surprise and fear
          Made me to quit the house.

2. GENTLEMAN That is the cause we trouble you so early;
          'Tis not our husbandry.

CERIMON   O, you say well.   20

1. GENTLEMAN But I much marvel that your lordship, having
          Rich tire about you, should at these early hours
          Shake off the golden slumber of repose.
          'Tis most strange
          Nature should be so conversant with pain,   25
          Being thereto not compell'd.

CERIMON   I held it ever
          Virtue and cunning were endowments greater
          Than nobleness and riches. Careless heirs
          May the two latter darken and expend;
          But immortality attends the former,   30
          Making a man a god. 'Tis known, I ever
          Have studied physic, through which secret art,
          By turning o'er authorities, I have,
          Together with my practice, made familiar
          To me and to my aid the blest infusions   35
          That dwell in vegetives, in metals, stones;
          And I can speak of the disturbances
          That nature works, and of her cures; which doth give me
          A more content in course of true delight
          Than to be thirsty after tottering honor,   40
          Or tie my treasure up in silken bags,
          To please the fool and death.

---

14. **standing bleak:** bare, desolate, exposed. 16. **principals:** rafters, support beams. 17. **topple:** fall down. 20. **husbandry:** habit. 22. **tire:** belongings. 25-26. **Nature should be so conversant with pain,/ Being thereto not compell'd:** Roughly, it is natural to care for people, so, even though I was unaffected by the storm, I did not sleep out of worry for others. 27-28. **Virtue and cunning were endowments greater/ Than nobleness and riches:** Roughly, I care more for learning than for money. 32. **secret art:** magical healing arts. 33. **authorities:** experts, ie. famed medical treatises; perhaps a reference to Rufus of Ephesus, a renowned Greek physician who wrote numerous medical treatises. On Ephesus, see line 43, below. 40. **thirsty after tottering honor:** Compare Cerimon's saintly life to those of the fawning courtiers of Pericles' court, or grasping Thaliard, or even, for that matter, the adventuring Pericles, who, in his travels, never finds space for spiritual reflection and growth. 42. **the fool and death:** the grinning, ergo, foolish skull of death.

2. GENTLEMAN	Your honor has through Ephesus pour'd forth
	Your charity, and hundreds call themselves
	Your creatures, who by you have been restor'd; 45
	And not your knowledge, your personal pain, but even
	Your purse, still open, hath built Lord Cerimon
	Such strong renown as time shall never raze.

Enter two or three [Servants] with a chest.

SERVANT	So, lift there.
CERIMON	What is that?
SERVANT	Sir, even now
	Did the sea toss up upon our shore this chest. 50
	'Tis of some wrack.
CERIMON	Set 't down; let's look upon't.
2. GENTLEMAN	'Tis like a coffin, sir.
CERIMON	Whate'er it be,
	'Tis wondrous heavy. Wrench it open straight.
	If the sea's stomach be o'ercharg'd with gold,
	'Tis a good constraint of fortune it belches upon us. 55
2. GENTLEMAN	'Tis so, my lord.
CERIMON	How close 'tis caulk'd and bitumed!
	Did the sea cast it up?
SERVANT	I never saw so huge a billow, sir,
	As toss'd it upon shore.
CERIMON	Wrench it open.
	Soft! It smells most sweetly in my sense. 60
2. GENTLEMAN	A delicate odor.
CERIMON	As ever hit my nostril. So, up with it!
	O you most potent gods! what's here? a corse!
1. GENTLEMAN	Most strange!
CERIMON	Shrouded in cloth of state; balm'd and entreasur'd 65
	With full bags of spices! A passport too!

---

43. **Ephesus:** in present day Turkey. 45. **creatures:** devoted followers. 45. **restor'd:** restored to health. 47. **Your purse, still open:** generosity. 48. **raze:** decay. 51. **wrack:** shipwreck. 53. **Wrench:** pry. 54. **sea's stomach:** from the depths of the sea, from its innards or belly. 58. **billow:** wave. 63. **corse:** corpse. 66. **full bags of spices:** A common practice to preserve the body. Ramsès II was embalmed with peppercorns up his nose. —**passport too:** A letter of instruction for her burial. The jewels are payment for land burial. The burial of the dead with money may also hearken to the Greco-Roman myth of Charon, the ferryman, who requires payment to tranport souls of the dead across the river Styx.

Apollo, perfect me in the characters!   [*Reads from a scroll.*]
   'Here I give to understand—
   If e'er this coffin drives aland—
   I, King Pericles, have lost   70
   This queen, worth all our mundane cost.
   Who finds her, give her burying;
   She was the daughter of a king.
   Besides this treasure for a fee,
   The gods requite his charity!'   75
If thou livest, Pericles, thou hast a heart
That even cracks for woe! This chanc'd tonight.

2. GENTLEMAN   Most likely, sir.

CERIMON   Nay, certainly tonight;
For look how fresh she looks! They were too rough
That threw her in the sea. Make a fire within.   80
Fetch hither all my boxes in my closet.   [*Exit a Servant.*]
Death may usurp on nature many hours,
And yet the fire of life kindle again
The o'erpress'd spirits. I heard of an Egyptian
That had nine hours lien dead,   85
Who was by good appliance recovered.

   Enter one with [boxes,] napkins, and fire.

Well said, well said! the fire and cloths.
The rough and woeful music that we have,
Cause it to sound, beseech you.   90
The viol once more. How thou stirr'st, thou block!†
The music there! I pray you give her air.
Gentlemen,
This queen will live; nature awakes; a warmth

---

67. **Apollo:** God of medicine and learning. —**perfect me in the characters:** Roughly, enable me the knowledge to read the (presumably foreign) script. 69. **drives aland:** comes ashore. 71. **mundane cost:** Roughly, all the gold in the world. 75. **requite:** reward. 77. **chanc'd:** happened. 79. **rough:** hasty. 81. **boxes:** his cures, which include the use of musical instruments. See line 89. 82. **usurp on:** rule over. 85. **lien:** lying. 86. **appliance:** the application of the proper medicine. 87. **Well said, well said:** Since the doctor was the last to speak, this line makes little sense. There may be some abridgement here. 89. **The rough and woeful music:** The use of music as a cure may have several sources. The ancient Pythagoreans used music as a means of curing and caring for the soul; in Greek myth, Orpheus, a musician, used his musical skills to enter into Hades and retrieve his beloved Eurydice. 91. **How thou stirr'st, thou block:** Said to the servant. Pay attention and follow my orders, you oaf. 92. **air:** room to breathe.

---

†   Clive Swift's Cerimon (BBC TV, 1984) revived Juliet Stevenson's Thaisa by simply rubbing her arms and then ordering that some music be performed. In director Phyllida Lloyd's 1994 production at the National Theatre, Kathryn Hunter's Cerimon was dressed as a "jigging witchdoctor with Fu Manchu whiskers" (Benedict Nightingale, "Swan of Avon as a dead duck." *The Times,* May 23, 1994).

Breathes out of her. She hath not been entranc'd   95
Above five hours. See how she 'gins to blow
Into life's flower again!

1. GENTLEMAN   The heavens,
Through you, increase our wonder, and set up
Your fame for ever.

CERIMON   She is alive! Behold,
Her eyelids, cases to those heavenly jewels   100
Which Pericles hath lost, begin to part
Their fringes of bright gold. The diamonds
Of a most praised water do appear
To make the world twice rich. Live, and make
Us weep to hear your fate, fair creature,   105
Rare as you seem to be!

                    She moves.

THAISA   O dear Diana,
Where am I? Where's my lord? What world is this?

2. GENTLEMAN Is not this strange?

1. GENTLEMAN Most rare.

CERIMON   Hush, my gentle neighbours!   110
Lend me your hands; to the next chamber bear her.
Get linen. Now this matter must be look'd to,
For her relapse is mortal. Come, come!
And Æsculapius guide us!   *They carry her away. Exeunt omnes.*

---

95. **entranc'd:** Perhaps, in a comma. 96. **'gins:** begins. 100-102. **heavenly jewels.. gold... diamonds:** in reference to her eyes. Note that, as in 3.2.26-42, Cerimon values life and learning as if it were gold. 106. **Diana:** Goddess of chastity. See 2.5.10. Her invocation here is a bit odd. Perhaps Shakespeare had in mind the old religion of Stregheria, which embraced goddess Diana as Queen of the Witches; witches, defined as wise women healers. 107. **Where am I? Where's my lord? What world is this?:** Corresponding to Gower's *Confessio Amantis*, BK VIII. 1214-1215. 111. **Lend me your hands:** Roughly, help me carry her. 113. **relapse is mortal:** Roughly, if she falls sick, she'll die. 114. **Æsculapius:** Son of Apollo, God of medicine, Æsculapius was killed by Zeus with a thunderbolt because he raised the dead. This may suggest the dark/cursed nature of Cerimon's "secret art." See 3.2.32.

SCENE III. [*Tharsus.* Cleon's *house.*]

Enter Pericles at Tharsus, with Cleon and Dionyza,
[and Lychorida with Marina in her arms].

PERICLES   Most honor'd Cleon, I must needs be gone.
My twelve months are expir'd, and Tyrus stands
In a litigious peace. You and your lady
Take from my heart all thankfulness! The gods
Make up the rest upon you!   5

CLEON   Your shafts of fortune, though they hurt you mortally,
Yet glance full wand'ringly on us.

DIONYZA   O your sweet queen!
That the strict Fates had pleas'd you had brought her hither
To have bless'd mine eyes with her!

PERICLES   We cannot but obey
The powers above us. Could I rage and roar   10
As doth the sea she lies in, yet the end
Must be as 'tis. My gentle babe Marina—whom,
For she was born at sea, I have nam'd so—here
I charge your charity withal, leaving her
The infant of your care; beseeching you   15
To give her princely training, that she may be
Manner'd as she is born.

CLEON   Fear not, my lord, but think
Your Grace, that fed my country with your corn,
For which the people's prayers still fall upon you,
Must in your child be thought on. If neglection   20
Should therein make me vile, the common body,
By you reliev'd, would force me to my duty.
But if to that my nature need a spur,
The gods revenge it upon me and mine
To the end of generation!

SCENE III.
1. **must needs:** need to be. 3. **litigious:** fragile. 5. **Make up the rest upon you:** Roughly, bless you.
6-7. **Your shafts of fortune, though they hurt you mortally,/ Yet glance full wand'ringly on us:**
Roughly, we share your pain. 8. **Fates:** Ironic, since the Fates measure not only the events of a life,
but also its length, which, in the case of Marina, Dionyza will attempt to cut short. 11. **she:** Thaisa.
12. **Marina:** From the Latin, *marinus*, of the sea. In Gower, her name is Thaise; in Twine it is Tharsia.
14. **withal:** in all things. 15. **beseeching:** urging. 17. **Manner'd as she is born:** Roughly, that she be
educated according to her station in life. 20. **neglection:** neglect of duty. 24. **The gods revenge it upon
me:** In Roman myth, this would be one god: Nemesis.

PERICLES	I believe you. 25
	Your honor and your goodness teach me to't
	Without your vows. Till she be married, madam,
	By bright Diana, whom we honor all,
	Unscissor'd shall this hair of mine remain,
	Though I show ill in't. So I take my leave. 30
	Good madam, make me blessed in your care
	In bringing up my child.
DIONYZA	I have one myself,
	Who shall not be more dear to my respect
	Than yours, my lord.
PERICLES	Madam, my thanks and prayers. 35
CLEON	We'll bring your Grace e'en to the edge o' th' shore,
	Then give you up to the mask'd Neptune and
	The gentlest winds of heaven.
PERICLES	I will embrace
	Your offer. Come, dearest madam. O, no tears,
	Lychorida, no tears! 40
	Look to your little mistress, on whose grace
	You may depend hereafter. Come, my lord. [*Exeunt.*]

SCENE IV. [*Ephesus. Cerimon's house.*]

Enter Cerimon and Thaisa.

CERIMON	Madam, this letter, and some certain jewels,
	Lay with you in your coffer; which are here
	At your command. Know you the character?
THAISA	It is my lord's.
	That I was shipp'd at sea I well remember, 5
	Even on my eaning time; but whether there
	Delivered, by the holy gods,
	I cannot rightly say. But since King Pericles,

---

26. **teach me to't:** make me believe it. 29. **Unscissor'd shall this hair of mine remain:** Obscure, though probably related to the myth of Medusa's hair. See 3.3.37, below. 33. **respect:** duty, attention. 37. **mask'd Neptune:** Obscure. Poseidon seduced Medusa, whose hair was turned to coiling snakes. After her death, her head became an apotropaic mask which both killed and redeemed. 42. **depend hereafter:** Roughly, Marina, when grown, will reward her nurse for her care.
SCENE IV.
2. **your coffer:** your coffin. 6. **eaning:** Related to the birth of sheep. Perhaps Shakespeare here means the birth of my little lamb. Alternatively, we might be dealing with a typo. The MS might have read "learning" or "bearing." 7. **Delivered:** had a child. Odd. Does she still think she is pregnant? If so, this indicates that the boy playing Thaisa appears with padding of some sort to fake pregnancy.

My wedded lord, I ne'er shall see again,
A vestal livery will I take me to,   10
And never more have joy.

CERIMON   Madam, if this you purpose as ye speak,
Diana's temple is not distant far,
Where you may abide until your date expire.
Moreover, if you please, a niece of mine   15
Shall there attend you.

THAISA   My recompense is thanks, that's all;
Yet my good will is great, though the gift small.   *Exeunt.*

ACT IV

Enter Gower.

GOWER   Imagine Pericles arriv'd at Tyre,
Welcom'd and settled to his own desire.
His woeful queen we leave at Ephesus,
Unto Diana there's a votaress.
Now to Marina bend your mind,   5
Whom our fast-growing scene must find
At Tharsus, and by Cleon train'd
In music, letters; who hath gain'd
Of education all the grace,
Which makes her both the heart and place   10
Of general wonder. But, alack,
That monster, Envy, oft the wrack
Of earned praise, Marina's life
Seeks to take off by treason's knife.

---

10. **vestal livery:** A devotee of Diana, see 2.5.10-11. Why Thaisa decides on not seeing Pericles again is mysterious. She may think him dead, but why not at least go back to Pentapolis? Thaisa, we later learn (5.3.77), does receive letters from her father's kingdom. So if a postal system exists, why not send word? In Gower, she believes her husband and child to be drowned (BK VIII: 1247). 14. **date expire:** Until you die. 18. **though the gift small:** Considering the jewels in the coffin, this line is a bit odd. Perhaps she means, I can never repay your kindness.

ACT IV.
2. **settled to his own desire:** Here, in reference to Pericles' self-willed fall into depression. 3. **woeful:** sad. 4. **votaress:** a follower, worshipper. 6. **fast-growing scene:** Moving forward/fast in time. See also line 4.48, below. 8. **letters:** learning. 12. **Envy:** Phthonos, the god of envy and jealousy; in Christianity, Envy is one of the Seven Deadly Sins. —**wrack:** ruin. 14. **Seeks to take off by treason's knife:** The envious Dionyza wants her dead.

And in this kind hath our Cleon   15
One daughter, and a wench full grown,
Even ripe for marriage rite. This maid
Hight Philoten; and it is said
For certain in our story, she
Would ever with Marina be.   20
Be't when she weav'd the sleided silk
With fingers long, small, white as milk;
Or when she would with sharp needle wound
The cambric, which she made more sound
By hurting it; or when to th' lute   25
She sung, and made the night-bird mute
That still records with moan; or when
She would with rich and constant pen
Vail to her mistress Dian; still
This Philoten contends in skill   30
With absolute Marina. So
With the dove of Paphos might the crow
Vie feathers white. Marina gets
All praises, which are paid as debts,
And not as given. This so darks   35
In Philoten all graceful marks
That Cleon's wife, with envy rare,
A present murder does prepare
For good Marina, that her daughter
Might stand peerless by this slaughter.   40
The sooner her vile thoughts to stead,
Lychorida, our nurse, is dead;
And cursed Dionyza hath
The pregnant instrument of wrath
Prest for this blow. The unborn event   45
I do commend to your content:
Only I carry winged time
Post on the lame feet of my rhyme;
Which never could I so convey

---

16. **wench:** woman. 18. **Hight Philoten:** Called Philoten, perhaps from the Greek *philein*, to love wisdom. In Gower, her name is Philotenne; in Twine, she is Philomacia. 21. **sleided:** fine. 24. **cambric:** fine, white linen. 25-31. **or when to th' lute…absolute Marina:** Roughly, no matter how wonderful she was, she was always a distant second to Marina. 32. **the dove of Paphos:** Doves are sacred to Aphrodite, who emerged from the sea at Paphos, Cyprus. 35. **darks:** blots, mars the beauty. 40. **peerless:** without competition, also playing upon her social position as peer of the realm. 41. **stead:** aid. 44. **pregnant:** ready, fully formed. 45. **Prest for this blow:** Pressed into service for this fatal blow. 47-48. **winged time/Post on the lame feet of my rhyme:** Playing upon poetic meter and the passage of time.

Unless your thoughts went on my way.   50
Dionyza does appear,
With Leonine, a murtherer.   *Exit.*

SCENE I. [*Tharsus. An open place near the seashore.*]

Enter Dionyza with Leonine.

DIONYZA   Thy oath remember; thou hast sworn to do't.
'Tis but a blow, which never shall be known.
Thou canst not do a thing in the world so soon
To yield thee so much profit. Let not conscience,
Which is but cold, inflaming love in thy bosom,   5
Inflame too nicely; nor let pity, which
Even women have cast off, melt thee, but be
A soldier to thy purpose.

LEONINE   I will do't.
But yet she is a goodly creature.

DIONYZA   The fitter then the gods should have her. Here   10
She comes weeping for her only mistress's death.
Thou art resolv'd?

LEONINE   I am resolv'd.

Enter Marina, with a basket of flowers.

MARINA   No, I will rob Tellus of her weed,
To strew thy green with flowers. The yellows, blues,   15
The purple violets, and marigolds,
Shall, as a carpet, hang upon thy grave
While summer days do last. Ay me, poor maid,
Born in a tempest when my mother died!
This world to me is like a lasting storm,   20
Whirring me from my friends.

DIONYZA   How now, Marina? Why do you keep alone?
How chance my daughter is not with you? Do not

---

52. **Leonine:** In Gower, his name is Theophilus. 52. **murtherer:** murderer.
SCENE I.
1. **to do't:** to murder Marina. 3-4. **Thou canst not do a thing in the world so soon/ To yield thee so much profit:** Roughly, you'll never make such easy money. 6. **too nicely:** fastidiously; roughly, don't give the murder too much thought. 11. **only mistress' death:** Lychorida. 12. **resolv'd:** firmly agreed. 14. **Tellus:** Ancient Roman goddess of the earth, Mother Earth. 15. **To strew thy green with flowers:** flowers over the green grass of the grave. 17. **carpet:** carpet of flowers.

Consume your blood with sorrowing. You have
A nurse of me. Lord, how your favor's chang'd   25
With this unprofitable woe! Come, come!
Give me your flowers. On the sea margent
Walk with Leonine. The air is quick there,
And it pierces and sharpens the stomach. Come,
Leonine, take her by the arm, walk with her.   30

MARINA   No, I pray you.
I'll not bereave you of your servant.

DIONYZA   Come, come!
I love the King your father, and yourself,
With more than foreign heart. We every day   35
Expect him here. When he shall come and find
Our paragon to all reports thus blasted,
He will repent the breadth of his great voyage;
Blame both my lord and me, that we have taken
No care to your best courses. Go, I pray you.   40
Walk, and be cheerful once again. Reserve
That excellent complexion which did steal
The eyes of young and old. Care not for me;
I can go home alone.

MARINA   Well, I will go;
But yet I have no desire to it.

DIONYZA   Come, come!   45
I know 'tis good for you.
Walk half an hour, Leonine, at the least.
Remember what I have said.

LEONINE   I warrant you, madam.

DIONYZA   I'll leave you, my sweet lady, for a while.
Pray walk softly; do not heat your blood.   50
What, I must have care of you.

MARINA   My thanks, sweet madam.   [Exit Dionyza.]
Is this wind westerly that blows?

LEONINE   Southwest.

---

24. **Consume your blood with sorrowing:** killing grief. 25. **favor's:** complexion has. 26. **unprofitable woe:** useless grieving. 28. **quick:** breezy, fresh. 29. **pierces and sharpens the stomach:** awakes the appetite. 32. **bereave:** rob, also playing upon her own sense of bereavement. 35. **more than foreign heart:** as if I were not a foreigner; with real affection for a sovereign king and his daughter. 37. **blasted:** ruined, ie. not as wondrously happy and fair as previously reported. 38. **breadth:** length. 42. **steal:** took, taken with. 50. **softly:** slowly.

MARINA   When I was born the wind was north.

LEONINE   Was't so?

MARINA   My father, as nurse says, did never fear,   55
            But cried "Good seamen!" to the sailors, galling
            His kingly hands hauling ropes;
            And, clasping to the mast, endur'd a sea
            That almost burst the deck.

LEONINE   When was this?

MARINA   When I was born.   60
            Never was waves nor wind more violent;
            And from the ladder tackle washes off
            A canvas climber. 'Ha!' says one, 'wolt out?'
            And with a dropping industry they skip
            From stem to stern. The boatswain whistles, and   .   65
            The master calls and trebles their confusion.

LEONINE   Come, say your prayers.

MARINA   What mean you?

LEONINE   If you require a little space for prayer,
            I grant it. Pray; but be not tedious, for   70
            The gods are quick of ear, and I am sworn
            To do my work with haste.

MARINA   Why will you kill me?

LEONINE   To satisfy my lady.

MARINA   Why would she have me kill'd?   75
            Now, as I can remember, by my troth,
            I never did her hurt in all my life.
            I never spake bad word nor did ill turn
            To any living creature. Believe me, la,
            I never kill'd a mouse, nor hurt a fly.   80
            I trod upon a worm against my will,
            But I wept for it. How have I offended
            Wherein my death might yield her any profit
            Or my life imply her any danger?

---

54. **wind was north:** See 3.47-48. 56. **galling:** chafing. 59. **burst the deck:** destroyed the ship. 63. **canvas climber:** a sailor on one of the mast sails. 63. **wolt out:** will out? Or, roughly, will we survive this? 64. **dropping:** dripping wet. 66. **trebles their confusion:** The constant orders triple their confusion. 69-70. **If you require a little space for prayer,/I grant it:** To prepare the soul for death. 78. **spake:** spoke. 81-82. **I trod upon a worm against my will,/But I wept for it:** A sign of Marina's innocence, but oddly comic.

LEONINE	My commission 85
	Is not to reason of the deed, but do't.
MARINA	You will not do't for all the world, I hope.
	You are well-favored, and your looks foreshow
	You have a gentle heart. I saw you lately
	When you caught hurt in parting two that fought. 90
	Good sooth, it show'd well in you. Do so now.
	Your lady seeks my life; come you between,
	And save poor me, the weaker.
LEONINE	I am sworn,
	And will dispatch. [*Seizes her.*]
	Enter Pirates.
1. PIRATE	Hold, villain! [*Leonine runs away.*] 95
2. PIRATE	A prize! a prize!
3. PIRATE	Half part, mates, half part! Come, let's have her aboard suddenly.
	Exeunt [*Pirates with Marina*].
	Enter Leonine.
LEONINE	These roguing thieves serve the great pirate Valdes,
	And they have seiz'd Marina. Let her go.
	There's no hope she will return. I'll swear she's dead 100
	And thrown into the sea. But I'll see further.
	Perhaps they will but please themselves upon her,
	Not carry her aboard. If she remain,
	Whom they have ravish'd must by me be slain. *Exit.*

---

94. **dispatch:** do my duty. 97. **Half part:** Roughly, we'll split this treasure, ransom her. 98. **Valdes:** Actually, the Admiral Diego Flores de Valdés was more of a pirate chaser. He was employed by the Spanish to chase off pirates from the coast of Brazil, and, later, to safeguard treasure coming from the Indies. 100. **I'll swear she's dead:** Echoing Thaliard at 1.3.25-26. 102. **please themselves upon her:** rape her.

SCENE II. [*Mytilene. A brothel.*]†

Enter Pander, Bawd, and Boult.

PANDER	Boult!
BOULT	Sir?
PANDER	Search the market narrowly. Mytilene is full of gallants. We lost too much money this mart by being too wenchless.
BAWD	We were never so much out of creatures. We have but poor 5 three, and they can do no more than they can do; and they with continual action are even as good as rotten.
PANDER	Therefore let's have fresh ones, whate'er we pay for them. If there be not a conscience to be us'd in every trade, we shall never prosper.
BAWD	Thou say'st true. 'Tis not our bringing up of poor bastards, as, I think, I have brought up some eleven— 11
BOULT	Ay, to eleven; and brought them down again. But shall I search the market?
BAWD	What else, man? The stuff we have, a strong wind will blow it to pieces, they are so pitifully sodden. 15
PANDER	Thou sayest true; they're too unwholesome, o' conscience. The poor Transylvanian is dead that lay with the little baggage.
BOULT	Ay, she quickly poop'd him; she made him roast meat for worms. But I'll go search the market. *Exit.*
PANDER	Three or four thousand chequins were as pretty a proportion to live quietly, and so give over. 21

SCENE II.
3. **narrowly:** carefully. —**gallants:** men, customers. 4. **too wenchless:** with no women working as prostitutes. 7. **continual action are even as good as rotten:** worn out and diseased. 8. **we pay for them:** The buying of a sex slave. 10. **poor bastards:** children of prostitutes. 12. **brought them down again:** Roughly, raised them into adulthood, then train them to be whores. 15. **sodden:** boiled, carnal/culinary wordplay playing upon stews, or whorehouses. 16. **unwholesome:** diseased. 17. **baggage:** prostitute. 18. **she quickly poop'd him; she made him roast meat for worms:** Roughly, she deceived him about her health and gave him a sexually transmitted disease. 20. **chequins:** gold coins.

---

† As the scene opened in David Thacker's 1989 RSC's production, diseased prostitutes retched and vomited into buckets (Peter Kemp, "Colour piece." *The Independent*, September 13, 1989). In a joint Royal Shakespeare Company and Cardboard Citizens production (dir. Adrian Jackson, 2003), the brothel was "tacky shed, with fairy lights on the terrace and a bloke in a satin suit outside; later, watching a couple move inside, you peer at them through rips in the red paper that covers the windows. As you do so, a video screen projects them in close-up and hugely enlarged on a wall" (Susannah Clapp, "And for my next trick…" *Observer*, July 27, 2003). In director Dominic Cooke's RSC production (2006), a Soho pole-dancing club represented the brothel in Mytilene (Benedict Nightingale, "*The Winter's Tale/Pericles.*" *The Times*, November 17, 2006).

BAWD	Why to give over, I pray you? Is it a shame to get when we are old?
PANDER	O, our credit comes not in like the commodity, nor the commodity wages not with the danger. Therefore, if in our youths we could pick up some pretty estate, 'twere not amiss to keep our door hatch'd. Besides, the sore terms we stand upon with the gods will be strong with us for giving o'er. 27
BAWD	Come, other sorts offend as well as we.
PANDER	As well as we? Ay, and better too. We offend worse. Neither is our profession any trade; it's no calling. But here comes Boult. 30

Enter Boult, with the Pirates and Marina.

BOULT	[*to Marina*] Come your ways.—My masters, you say she's a virgin?
SAILOR	O, sir, we doubt it not.
BOULT	Master, I have gone through for this piece you see. If you like her, so; if not, I have lost my earnest.
BAWD	Boult, has she any qualities? 35
BOULT	She has a good face, speaks well, and has excellent good clothes. There's no farther necessity of qualities can make her be refus'd.
BAWD	What's her price, Boult?
BOULT	I cannot be bated one doit of a thousand pieces. 39
PANDER	Well, follow me, my masters; you shall have your money presently. Wife, take her in; instruct her what she has to do, that she may not be raw in her entertainment. [*Exeunt Pander and Pirates.*]
BAWD	Boult, take you the marks of her—the color of her hair, complexion, height, her age, with warrant of her virginity; and cry, "He that will give most shall have her first." Such a maidenhead were no cheap thing, if men were as they have been. Get this done as I command you.
BOULT	Performance shall follow. *Exit.*
MARINA	Alack that Leonine was so slack, so slow!
	He should have struck, not spoke; or that these pirates, 50
	Not enough barbarous, had not o'erboard thrown me
	For to seek my mother!

---

26. **hatch'd:** closed. —**sore terms:** bad term but also playing upon venereal sores. See 4.2.7 and 14-17, above. 27. **giving o'er:** quit this line of work. 33. **this piece:** objectified piece of flesh. 34. **earnest:** skill, ability to pick a good prostitute. 35. **qualities:** skills, attributes. 37. **There's no farther necessity of qualities can make her be refus'd:** Roughly, there is no reason why a man would turn her down. 39. **I cannot be bated one doit:** Roughly, I won't take a penny less. 42. **raw in her entertainment:** inexperienced in satisfying her clients. 43. **the marks of her:** make a description of her. 45-46. **maidenhead were no cheap thing:** The plan is to sell her virginity to the highest bidder. 52. **For to seek my mother:** Roughly, I wish I were drowned like my mother.

BAWD	Why lament you, pretty one?	
MARINA	That I am pretty.	
BAWD	Come, the gods have done their part in you.	55
MARINA	I accuse them not.	
BAWD	You are light into my hands, where you are like to live.	
MARINA	The more my fault To scape his hands where I was like to die.	
BAWD	Ay, and you shall live in pleasure.	60
MARINA	No.	
BAWD	Yes, indeed shall you, and taste gentlemen of all fashions. You shall fare well; you shall have the difference of all complexions. What, do you stop your ears?	
MARINA	Are you a woman?	65
BAWD	What would you have me be, an I be not a woman?	
MARINA	An honest woman, or not a woman.	
BAWD	Marry whip thee, gosling! I think I shall have something to do with you. Come, you're a young foolish sapling, and must be bowed as I would have you.	70
MARINA	The gods defend me!	
BAWD	If it please the gods to defend you by men, then men must comfort you, men must feed you, men must stir you up. Boult's return'd.	

Enter Boult.

	Now, sir, hast thou cried her through the market?	
BOULT	I have cried her almost to the number of her hairs; I have drawn her picture with my voice.	76
BAWD	And I prithee tell me, how dost thou find the inclination of the people, especially of the younger sort?	

---

54. **That I am pretty:** Marina's dilemma echoes Clare's in George Wilkins' *Miseries of an Enforced Marriage* (1607): "yet for all this, who ere shall marry mee/ I am but his whore, live in Adultery./ I cannot step into the path of pleasure/For which I was created, bourne unto,/ Let me live nere so honest, rich or poor,/ If I once wed, yet I must live a whore./ I must be made a strumpet gainst my will" (lines 821-827). 55. **have done their part in you:** have made you lovely. 60. **pleasure:** sexual activity. 62. **taste:** relating sex to appetite. 63. **difference of all complexions:** a vast variety of customers who will have sex with you. 62-63. **Yes, indeed shall you, and taste gentlemen of all fashions. You shall fare well; you shall have the difference of all complexions:** Echoing George Wilkins' *Miseries of Enforced Marriage* (1607): "thou must be acquainted with all sorts of men" (lines 20-21). 66. **an I be not:** if I am not. 68. **gosling:** prude. 69. **must be bowed:** made flexible, pliant, loose, whorish. 73. **men must stir you up:** excite you sexually. 75. **cried her:** advertised her availability. 77. **inclination:** interest.

| BOULT | Faith, they listened to me as they would have hearkened to their father's testament. There was a Spaniard's mouth so wat'red! and he went to bed to her very description. | 81 |

BOULT — Faith, they listened to me as they would have hearkened to their father's testament. There was a Spaniard's mouth so wat'red! and he went to bed to her very description. 81

BAWD — We shall have him here tomorrow with his best ruff on.

BOULT — Tonight, tonight! But, mistress, do you know the French knight that cow'rs i' the hams?

BAWD — Who, Monsieur Verollus? 85

BOULT — Ay, he. He offered to cut a caper at the proclamation; but he made a groan at it, and swore he would see her tomorrow.

BAWD — Well, well; as for him, he brought his disease hither: here he does but repair it. I know he will come in our shadow, to scatter his crowns in the sun. 90

BOULT — Well, if we had of every nation a traveller, we should lodge them with this sign.

BAWD — [to Marina] Pray you come hither awhile. You have fortunes coming upon you. Mark me: you must seem to do that fearfully which you commit willingly, despise profit where you have most gain. To weep that you live as ye do makes pity in your lovers. Seldom but that pity begets you a good opinion, and that opinion a mere profit.

MARINA — I understand you not. 99

BOULT — O, take her home, mistress, take her home! These blushes of hers must be quench'd with some present practice.

BAWD — Thou sayest true, i'faith; so they must; for your bride goes to that with shame which is her way to go with warrant.

BOULT — Faith, some do, and some do not. But, mistress, if I have bargain'd for the joint— 105

BAWD — Thou mayst cut a morsel off the spit?

BOULT — I may so.

---

79. **hearkened:** heard. 80-81. **he went to bed to her very description:** imagined himself in bed with her. 82. **ruff:** an elaborate Elizabethan/Jacobean collar. 84. **cow'rs:** walks unsteadily. Echoing, albeit faintly, George Wilkins' *Miseries of Enforced Marriage* (1607): "I saw a leane fellow, with sunke eyes, and shamble legges, sigh pitifully" (lines 501-502). 85. **Monsieur Verollus:** Mister Syphilis. 86. **cut a caper:** danced merrily. 88. **disease:** sexually transmitted disease. 89-90. **his crowns in the sun:** to throw his money around. 93-94. **fortunes coming upon you:** money, good luck, lots of business. 94-95. **you must seem to do that fearfully which you commit willingly:** Pretend you hate prostitution. 101. **quench'd with some present practice:** She has to be schooled in the arts of her trade, though she can't be violated, as her main selling point is her virginity. 104-106. **bargain'd for the joint—/ Thou mayst cut a morsel off the spit:** Roughly, I want a piece of her as well. Her body as a sexual leftover.

BAWD	Who should deny it? Come, young one, I like the manner of your garments well.
BOULT	Ay, by my faith, they shall not be chang'd yet. 110
BAWD	Boult, spend thou that in the town. Report what a sojourner we have; you'll lose nothing by custom. When Nature fram'd this piece, she meant thee a good turn. Therefore say what a paragon she is, and thou hast the harvest out of thine own report.
BOULT	I warrant you, mistress, thunder shall not so awake the beds of eels as my giving out her beauty stirs up the lewdly inclined. I'll bring home some tonight.
BAWD	Come your ways, follow me.
MARINA	If fires be hot, knives sharp, or waters deep, Untied I still my virgin knot will keep. 120 Diana aid my purpose!
BAWD	What have we to do with Diana? Pray you, will you go with us? *Exeunt.*

SCENE III. [*Tharsus. Cleon's house.*]

Enter Cleon and Dionyza.

DIONYZA	Why are you foolish? Can it be undone?
CLEON	O Dionyza, such a piece of slaughter The sun and moon ne'er look'd upon!
DIONYZA	I think you'll turn a child again.
CLEON	Were I chief lord of all this spacious world, 5 I'd give it to undo the deed. O lady, Much less in blood than virtue, yet a princess To equal any single crown o' th' earth I' th' justice of compare! O villain Leonine! Whom thou hast pois'ned too. 10 If thou hadst drunk to him, 't had been a kindness

---

111. **sojourner:** visitor, Marina is newly arrived; playing also upon *sovereign*, valuable coin, treasure. 115. **awake the beds of eels:** eels stir like snakes, compared to excited phalluses stirring with the promise of sexual activity. 119-20. **If fires be hot, knives sharp, or waters deep/ Untied I still my virgin knot will keep:** Roughly, no matter the torture, I'll keep my virginity.
SCENE III.
4. **think you'll turn a child again:** Roughly, you're acting like a baby. 5. **chief lord of all this spacious world:** king of the world. 6-7. **O lady,/Much less in blood than virtue:** A lady in rank but not in action. 11. **If thou hadst drunk to him, 't had been a kindness:** If you had drank poison, rather than poisoned his mind.

Becoming well thy fact. What canst thou say
When noble Pericles shall demand his child?

DIONYZA   That she is dead. Nurses are not the Fates,
To foster it, nor ever to preserve.   15
She died at night; I'll say so. Who can cross it?
Unless you play the pious innocent
And for an honest attribute cry out
"She died by foul play."

CLEON   O, go to! Well, well,
Of all the faults beneath the heavens, the gods   20
Do like this worst.

DIONYZA   Be one of those that think
The petty wrens of Tharsus will fly hence
And open this to Pericles. I do shame
To think of what a noble strain you are,
And of how coward a spirit.

CLEON   To such proceeding   25
Who ever but his approbation added,
Though not his prime consent, he did not flow
From honorable sources.

DIONYZA   Be it so, then.
Yet none does know but you how she came dead,
Nor none can know, Leonine being gone.   30
She did distain my child and stood between
Her and her fortunes. None would look on her,
But cast their gazes on Marina's face,
Whilst ours was blurted at, and held a mawkin,
Not worth the time of day. It pierc'd me thorough;   35
And though you call my course unnatural,
You not your child well loving, yet I find
It greets me as an enterprise of kindness
Perform'd to your sole daughter.

CLEON   Heavens forgive it!

DIONYZA   And as for Pericles,   40
What should he say? We wept after her hearse,

---

14. **the Fates:** See 3.3.8. 16. **cross:** contradict. 20. **faults:** sins. 22. **wrens:** birds; see 4.3.46-48, below. 24-25. **To think of what a noble strain you are,/ And of how coward a spirit:** Nobility was thought to derive from the brave exploits of one's ancestors. 25-28. **To such proceeding...From honorable sources:** Obscure. Perhaps, you did it with good intentions. 31. **She did distain my child:** There is no evidence for this accusation. 34. **Whilst ours was blurted at, and held a mawkin:** considered second-rate. 35. **It pierc'd me thorough:** Cut me deeply. 41. **hearse:** funeral hearse.

And yet we mourn. Her monument
Is almost finish'd, and her epitaphs
In glitt'ring golden characters express
A general praise to her, and care in us   45
At whose expense 'tis done.

CLEON   Thou art like the harpy,
Which, to betray, dost, with thine angel's face,
Seize with thine eagle's talents.

DIONYZA   You are like one that superstitiously
Doth swear to th' gods that winter kills the flies;   50
But yet I know you'll do as I advise.   *Exeunt.*

SCENE IV. [*Before the monument of Marina at Tharsus.*]

Enter Gower.

GOWER   Thus time we waste and longest leagues make short;
Sail seas in cockles, have and wish but for't;
Making, to take your imagination,
From bourn to bourn, region to region.
By you being pardoned, we commit no crime   5
To use one language in each several clime
Where our scenes seem to live. I do beseech you
To learn of me, who stand i' th' gaps to teach you,
The stages of our story. Pericles
Is now again thwarting the wayward seas,   10
Attended on by many a lord and knight,
To see his daughter, all his live's delight.
Old Helicanus goes along. Behind
Is left to govern it, you bear in mind,
Old Escanes, whom Helicanus late   15

---

46. **At whose expense:** Cleon and Dionyza have paid for the funeral. 46-48. **harpy,/....thine angel's face,/ Seize with thine eagle's talents:** Monsters of Greek myth, sometimes associated with the Sirens. Half woman, half predatory bird. —**talents:** talons, claws. 50. **winter kills the flies:** Roughly, don't mourn or pray to the gods for what is done; accept the inevitable.

SCENE IV.

1. **leagues:** distances of the water or sea. 2. **Sail seas in cockles:** sails, rounded like cockle shells. 6. **several clime:** various locations; Ben Jonson famously ridiculed the Chorus in *Pericles* as a device that wafts the audience over the seas from one city to another. 8. **i' th' gaps:** the parts of the story that are summarized, rather than acted. 10. **wayward seas:** willful, disobedient. In Shakespeare, usually applied to children, here perhaps in reference to Palaemon, a youthful sea-god who came to the aid of sailors in distress. 12. **all his live's delight:** Difficult to believe, since he had not seen Marina since the day she was born. 15. **Old Escanes:** It is odd that Escanes, seen briefly in 2.4, is mentioned; a sign of abridgement?

Advanc'd in time to great and high estate.
Well-sailing ships and bounteous winds have brought
This king to Tharsus—think his pilot thought;
So with his steerage shall your thoughts grow on—
To fetch his daughter home, who first is gone.   20
Like motes and shadows see them move awhile.
Your ears unto your eyes I'll reconcile.

                                        [*Dumb Show.*]

Enter Pericles, at one door, with all his Train; Cleon and Dionyza at the other. Cleon
shows Pericles the tomb [of Marina], whereat Pericles makes lamentation, puts on
sackcloth, and in a mighty passion departs. [Then exeunt Cleon, Dionyza, and the rest.]

See how belief may suffer by foul show!
This borrowed passion stands for true old woe;
And Pericles, in sorrow all devour'd,   25
With sighs shot through and biggest tears o'ershow'r'd,
Leaves Tharsus and again embarks. He swears
Never to wash his face nor cut his hairs.
He puts on sackcloth, and to sea. He bears
A tempest which his mortal vessel tears,   30
And yet he rides it out. Now please you wit
The epitaph is for Marina writ
By wicked Dionyza.   [*Reads the inscription.*]
          The fairest, sweet'st, and best lies here,
          Who withered in her spring of year.   35
          She was of Tyrus the King's daughter,
          On whom foul death hath made this slaughter;
          Marina was she call'd, and at her birth,
          Thetis, being proud, swallowed some part o' th' earth.
          Therefore the earth, fearing to be o'erflowed,   40
          Hath Thetis' birth-child on the heavens bestowed;
          Wherefore she does (and swears she'll never stint)
          Make raging battery upon shores of flint.

---

18. **think his pilot thought:** Think that he can move from place to place but with your thoughts. See 3.57-58. 20. **To fetch his daughter home:** Pericles has come for his daughter, not knowing that she is, according to Cleon and his wife, suddenly dead. 23. **foul:** false. 24. **This borrowed passion:** Cleon and Dionyza's false mourning. 25. **all devour'd:** consumed by grief. 28. **Never to wash his face nor cut his hairs:** Pericles has already sworn not to cut his hair, so the detail is inexplicable. See 3.3.27-29. 29. **sackcloth:** Common mourning clothes. 30. **mortal vessel:** Pericles' body, which has voyaged over a sea/life of pain/tears. 35. **spring of year:** youth. 39. **Thetis, being proud, swallowed some part o' th' earth:** Confused. Thetis was a sea nymph and mother to Achilles. Shakespeare means Tethys, wife of Oceanus, lord of the Oceans, not to be confused with Poseidon, who ruled over the Mediterranean only. 43. **raging battery:** relentless attack.

No visor does become black villany
So well as soft and tender flattery.   45
Let Pericles believe his daughter's dead
And bear his courses to be ordered
By Lady Fortune, while our scene must play
His daughter's woe and heavy well-a-day
In her unholy service. Patience then,   50
And think you now are all in Mytilen.   *Exit.*

SCENE V. [*Mytilene. A street before the brothel.*]

Enter two Gentlemen [from the brothel].

1. GENTLEMAN Did you ever hear the like?

2. GENTLEMAN No, nor never shall do in such a place as this, she being once gone.

1. GENTLEMAN But to have divinity preach'd there!
Did you ever dream of such a thing?

2. GENTLEMAN No, no. Come, I am for no more bawdy houses. Shall's go hear   5
the Vestals sing?

1. GENTLEMAN I'll do anything now that is virtuous, but I am out of the road of
rutting for ever.   *Exeunt.*

SCENE VI. [*Mytilene. A room in the brothel.*]

Enter [Pander, Bawd, and Boult].

PANDER   Well, I had rather than twice the worth of her she had ne'er come
here.

BAWD   Fie, fie upon her! she's able to freeze the god Priapus and undo
a whole generation. We must either get her ravished or be rid of
her. When she should do for clients her fitment, and do me the
kindness of our profession, she has me her quirks, her reasons,
her master reasons, her prayers, her knees, that she would make a

---

44-45. **No visor does become black villainy/ So well as soft and tender flattery:** Roughly, nothing
can blind us to the truth so easily as a tender lie. 47. **courses:** his destiny. 49. **well-a-day:** grief. 50.
unholy service: the saintly Marina prostituted.
SCENE V.
3. **there:** in a whorehouse. 5. **bawdy houses:** whorehouses. 6. **Vestals:** virgins, nuns. 7-8. **road of
rutting:** habit of sleeping with prostitutes.
SCENE VI.
3. **freeze the god Priapus and undo a whole generation:** Unintentionally comic. Priapus, a male god
of fertility remarkable for his hard phallus. Freeze here meaning, cold, deadened. 4. **ravished:** raped.

	Puritan of the devil if he should cheapen a kiss of her.	
BOULT	Faith, I must ravish her, or she'll disfurnish us of all our cavaliers and make our swearers priests.	10
PANDER	Now the pox upon her greensickness for me!	
BAWD	Faith, there's no way to be rid on't but by the way to the pox. Here comes the Lord Lysimachus disguised.	
BOULT	We should have both lord and lown if the peevish baggage would but give way to customers.	15

Enter Lysimachus.

LYSIMACHUS	How now? How a dozen of virginities?	
BAWD	Now the gods to bless your Honor!	
BOULT	I am glad to see your Honor in good health.	
LYSIMACHUS	You may so; 'tis the better for you that your resorters stand upon sound legs. How now, wholesome iniquity? Have you that a man may deal withal and defy the surgeon?	21
BAWD	We have here one, sir, if she would—but there never came her like in Mytilene.	
LYSIMACHUS	If she'd do the deed of darkness, thou wouldst say.	
BAWD	Your Honor knows what 'tis to say well enough.	25
LYSIMACHUS	Well, call forth, call forth.	
BOULT	For flesh and blood, sir, white and red, you shall see a rose; and she were a rose indeed, if she had but—	
LYSIMACHUS	What, prithee?	
BOULT	O, sir, I can be modest.	30
LYSIMACHUS	That dignifies the renown of a bawd, no less than it gives a good report to a number to be chaste. [*Exit Boult.*]	

---

9. **disfurnish:** deprive. —**cavaliers:** phallic pun on rapier-danglers, customers. 11. **greensickness:** squeamishness. 12. **to the pox:** by giving her a sexual disease. 14. **lown:** lowborn. —**baggage:** whore. 15.*sd*. **Lysimachus:** In Gower, his name is Atenagoras; in Twine's version, he is a young widower with a daughter. 16. **How a dozen of virginities:** How much for a dozen virgins? They are clearly old friends. 20. **sound legs:** physically, firm, fertile. —**wholesome iniquity:** ironic address to a bawd. 21. **defy the surgeon:** escape the need of a surgeon; ie. a whore without a disease. 24. **deed of darkness:** sexual congress. 28. **rose indeed, if she had but:** Roughly, Marina would be a rose if she had no thorns, no pricks of conscience, playing also upon pricks and penis, rose as vagina. Also faintly echoing George Wilkins' *Miseries of Enforced Marriage* (1607): "Let them be what Flowers they will, and they were Roses, I will plucke none of them for pricking my fingers" (lines 162-163).

BAWD	Here comes that which grows to the stalk—never pluck'd yet, I can assure you.
	Enter [Boult with] Marina.
	Is she not a fair creature? 35
LYSIMACHUS	Faith, she would serve after a long voyage at sea. Well, there's for you. Leave us. [*Gives money.*]
BAWD	I beseech your Honor give me leave a word, and I'll have done presently.
LYSIMACHUS	I beseech you do. 40
BAWD	[*to Marina*] First, I would have you note this is an honorable man.
MARINA	I desire to find him so, that I may worthily note him.
BAWD	Next, he's the governor of this country, and a man whom I am bound to.
MARINA	If he govern the country, you are bound to him indeed; but how honorable he is in that, I know not. 46
BAWD	Pray you, without any more virginal fencing, will you use him kindly? He will line your apron with gold.
MARINA	What he will do graciously, I will thankfully receive.
LYSIMACHUS	Ha' you done? 50
BAWD	My lord, she's not pac'd yet; you must take some pains to work her to your manage.—Come, we will leave his honor and her together.—Go thy ways. *Exeunt Bawd, [Pander, and Boult].*
LYSIMACHUS	Now, pretty one, how long have you been at this trade?
MARINA	What trade, sir? 55
LYSIMACHUS	Why, I cannot name't but I shall offend.
MARINA	I cannot be offended with my trade. Please you to name it.
LYSIMACHUS	How long have you been of this profession?
MARINA	E'er since I can remember.
LYSIMACHUS	Did you go to't so young? Were you a gamester at five, or at seven?
MARINA	Earlier too, sir, if now I be one. 61
LYSIMACHUS	Why, the house you dwell in proclaims you to be a creature of sale.

---

33. **never pluck'd:** viriginal, unplucked flower. 41. **honorable:** rich, important. 42. **desire:** hope. 47. **virginal fencing:** attempts to parry, defend virginity. 51. **pac'd yet:** broken in, trained. 54. **trade:** prostitution. 60. **gamester:** prostitute.

MARINA	Do you know this house to be a place of such resort, and will come into't? I hear say you're of honorable parts, and are the governor of this place. 65
LYSIMACHUS	Why, hath your principal made known unto you who I am?
MARINA	Who is my principal?
LYSIMACHUS	Why, your herb-woman, she that sets seeds and roots of shame and iniquity. O, you have heard something of my power, and so stand aloof for more serious wooing. But I protest to thee, pretty one, my authority shall not see thee, or else look friendly upon thee. Come, bring me to some private place. Come, come!
MARINA	If you were born to honor, show it now; If put upon you, make the judgment good That thought you worthy of it. 75
LYSIMACHUS	How's this? how's this? Some more; be sage.
MARINA	For me, That am a maid, though most ungentle fortune Have plac'd me in this sty, where, since I came, Diseases have been sold dearer than physic— O that the gods 80 Would set me free from this unhallowed place, Though they did change me to the meanest bird That flies i' th' purer air!
LYSIMACHUS	I did not think Thou couldst have spoke so well; ne'er dreamt thou couldst. Had I brought hither a corrupted mind, 85 Thy speech had altered it. Hold, here's gold for thee. Persever in that clear way thou goest, And the gods strengthen thee!
MARINA	The good gods preserve you!
LYSIMACHUS	For me, be you thoughten That I came with no ill intent; for to me 90 The very doors and windows savor vilely. Fare thee well. Thou art a piece of virtue, and I doubt not but thy training hath been noble.

66. **principal:** pimp. 68. **herb-woman:** a woman who helps plant seed, sperm; a pimp. 73. **honor:** ethics. 76. **sage:** sagacious, wise, well-spoken. 78. **sty:** whorehouse, where customers rut like pigs. 81. **unhallowed:** unwholesome, diseased, sinful. 82. **change me to the meanest bird:** In Greek myth, Procne was transformed into a swallow, and her sister Philomel was turned into a nightingale. 85. **corrupted:** sinful. 89. **be you thoughten:** Roughly, I hope you think. 90. **That I came with no ill intent:** Considering his demand that she sleep with him, this is difficult to explain. 91. **savor vilely:** suggesting inequity, scummy.

Hold, here's more gold for thee.
A curse upon him, die he like a thief,   95
That robs thee of thy goodness! If thou dost
Hear from me, it shall be for thy good.

[Enter Boult.]

BOULT   I beseech your Honor, one piece for me.

LYSIMACHUS   Avaunt thou damned doorkeeper!
Your house, but for this virgin that doth prop it,   100
Would sink, and overwhelm you. Away!   *[Exit.]*

BOULT   How's this? We must take another course with you! If your peevish
chastity, which is not worth a breakfast in the cheapest country
under the cope, shall undo a whole household, let me be gelded
like a spaniel. Come your ways.   105

MARINA   Whither would you have me?

BOULT   I must have your maidenhead taken off, or the common hangman
shall execute it. Come your ways. We'll have no more gentlemen
driven away. Come your ways, I say.

Enter Bawd.

BAWD   How now? What's the matter?   110

BOULT   Worse and worse, mistress. She has here spoken holy words to the
Lord Lysimachus.

BAWD   O abominable!

BOULT   She makes our profession as it were to stink afore the face of the
gods.   115

BAWD   Marry hang her up for ever!

BOULT   The nobleman would have dealt with her like a nobleman, and she
sent him away as cold as a snowball; saying his prayers too.

BAWD   Boult, take her away; use her at thy pleasure. Crack the glass of her
virginity and make the rest malleable.   120

BOULT   An if she were a thornier piece of ground than she is, she shall be
ploughed.

---

96. **goodness:** virtue and virginity. 98. **one piece:** one piece of gold. 99. **Avaunt:** avoid me. 101. **sink:**
weighed down by sin. 102-104. **We must take another course with you! If your peevish chastity,
which is not worth a breakfast in the cheapest country under the cope:** Roughly, if your virginity
is making us poor, you must be robbed of it. 107. **hangman:** who cuts off heads; pun on maidenheads/
virginity. 111. **holy words:** thus, non-erotic. 118. **cold as a snowball:** See 4.6.3. 119-120. **the glass of
her virginity:** her hymen. 121. **thornier:** difficult, unreceptive, unwilling. 122. **ploughed:** planted with
male seed, sperm.

MARINA	Hark, hark, you gods!
BAWD	She conjures. Away with her! Would she had never come within my doors!—Marry hang you!—She's born to undo us.—Will you not go the way of womenkind? Marry come up, my dish of chastity with rosemary and bays! *Exit.*
BOULT	Come, mistress; come your ways with me.
MARINA	Whither wilt thou have me?
BOULT	To take from you the jewel you hold so dear. 130
MARINA	Prithee tell me one thing first.
BOULT	Come now, your one thing.
MARINA	What canst thou wish thine enemy to be?
BOULT	Why, I could wish him to be my master, or rather my mistress.
MARINA	Neither of these are so bad as thou art, 135 Since they do better thee in their command. Thou hold'st a place for which the pained'st fiend Of hell would not in reputation change. Thou art the damned doorkeeper to every Coistrel that comes enquiring for his Tib. 140 To the choleric fisting of every rogue Thy ear is liable. Thy food is such As hath been belch'd on by infected lungs.
BOULT	What would you have me do? go to the wars, would you? where a man may serve seven years for the loss of a leg, and have not money enough in the end to buy him a wooden one?
MARINA	Do anything but this thou doest. Empty Old receptacles, or common shores, of filth; Serve by indenture to the common hangman. Any of these ways are yet better than this; 150 For what thou professest, a baboon, could he speak, Would own a name too dear. O that the gods Would safely deliver me from this place!

---

127. **rosemary and bays:** herbs, see 4.6.68. 130. **the jewel:** her chastity. 137. **pained'st fiend:** devil of hell; burning in pain, hence, venereal disease. 140. **Coistrel that comes enquiring for his Tib:** Roughly, a John that comes looking for his whore. 141-143. **choleric fisting...infected lungs:** diseased coughing. 144-146. **What would you have me do? go to the wars, would you? where a man may serve seven years for the loss of a leg, and have not money enough in the end to buy him a wooden one:** For a comic scene, Boult's reply, that he, like Marina, is a victim of circumstance, has an unexpected degree of realism. 148. **Old receptacles, or common shores, of filth:** Roughly, clean outhouses and sewers. 151. **baboon:** A sign of degeneracy, bestiality.

Here, here's gold for thee.
If that thy master would gain by me,   155
Proclaim that I can sing, weave, sew, and dance,
With other virtues, which I'll keep from boast;
And I will undertake all these to teach.
I doubt not but this populous city will
Yield many scholars.   160

BOULT   But can you teach all this you speak of?

MARINA   Prove that I cannot, take me home again
And prostitute me to the basest groom
That doth frequent your house.

BOULT   Well, I will see what I can do for thee.   165
If I can place thee, I will.

MARINA   But amongst honest women.

BOULT   Faith, my acquaintance lies little amongst them. But since my
master and mistress have bought you, there's no going but by their
consent. Therefore I will make them acquainted with your purpose,
and I doubt not but I shall find them tractable enough. Come, I'll
do for thee what I can. Come your ways.   *Exeunt.*

ACT V

Enter Gower.

GOWER   Marina thus the brothel scapes and chances
Into an honest house, our story says.
She sings like one immortal, and she dances
As goddess-like to her admired lays;
Deep clerks she dumbs; and with her neele composes   5
Nature's own shape of bud, bird, branch, or berry,
That even her art sisters the natural roses;
Her inkle, silk, twin with the rubied cherry;
That pupils lacks she none of noble race,

---

163. **prostitute me to the basest groom:** Marina's dare is out of keeping with her innocence. In offering
the bargain, she has, at least on some level, contemplated a life of prostitution.
ACT V.
1. **scapes and chances:** escapes and is luckily placed. 4. **lays:** songs. 5. **Deep clerks she dumbs:**
Roughly, the educated are dumbfounded. —**neele:** needle. 7. **sisters:** duplicates, playing on the idea of
a twin sister; see next line. 8. **inkle:** yarn.

Who pour their bounty on her; and her gain   10
She gives the cursed bawd. Here we her place;
And to her father turn our thoughts again.
Where we left him on the sea, we there him lost;
Whence, driven before the winds, he is arriv'd
Here where his daughter dwells; and on this coast   15
Suppose him now at anchor. The city striv'd
God Neptune's annual feast to keep; from whence
Lysimachus our Tyrian ship espies,
His banners sable, trimm'd with rich expense,
And to him in his barge with fervor hies.   20
In your supposing once more put your sight
Of heavy Pericles. Think this his bark,
Where what is done in action (more, if might)
Shall be discover'd—please you sit and hark.   *Exit.*

SCENE I. [*On board Pericles' ship, off Mytilene. A pavilion on deck, with a curtain before it; Pericles within it, on a couch. A barge lying beside the Tyrian vessel.*]

Enter Helicanus; to him two Sailors, [one belonging to the Tyrian vessel, the other to the barge].

1. SAILOR	[to the Sailor of Mytilene] Where is
	Lord Helicane? He can resolve you.
	O, here he is.
	Sir, there is a barge put off from Mytilene,
	And in it is Lysimachus the Governor, 5
	Who craves to come aboard. What is your will?
HELICANUS	That he have his. Call up some gentlemen.
1. SAILOR	Ho, gentlemen! my lord calls.

Enter two or three Gentlemen.

1. GENTLEMAN	Doth your lordship call?
HELICANUS	Gentlemen, there is some of worth would come aboard. 10
	I pray ye greet them fairly.[*Exeunt Gentlemen and the two Sailors.*]

Enter [from the barge] Lysimachus [and Lords, with the Gentlemen and the two Sailors].

---

10. **pour their bounty on her:** she is well paid for her arts. 11. **we her place:** leave her for a while. 16. **Suppose him now at anchor:** Imagine his ship anchored in the harbor. 17. **God Neptune's annual feast:** The Poseidean feasts were celebrated with the sacrifice of bulls. 18. **espies:** sees. 20. **fervor hies:** with zeal goes.
SCENE I.
6. **craves:** desires, asks to. 9. **Doth:** does.

1. SAILOR	Sir, this is the man that can, in aught you would, Resolve you.
LYSIMACHUS	Hail, reverent sir! the gods preserve you!
HELICANUS	And you, sir, to outlive the age I am, And die as I would do.

LYSIMACHUS   You wish me well.   15
Being on shore, honoring of Neptune's triumphs,
Seeing this goodly vessel ride before us,
I made to it, to know of whence you are.

HELICANUS   First, what is your place?

LYSIMACHUS   I am the Governor
Of this place you lie before.   20

HELICANUS   Sir,
Our vessel is of Tyre, in it the King;
A man who for this three months hath not spoken
To any one, nor taken sustenance
But to prorogue his grief.   25

LYSIMACHUS   Upon what ground is his distemperature?

HELICANUS   'Twould be too tedious to repeat;
But the main grief springs from the loss
Of a beloved daughter and a wife.

LYSIMACHUS   May we not see him?

HELICANUS   You may;   30
But bootless is your sight. He will not speak
To any.

LYSIMACHUS   Yet let me obtain my wish.

HELICANUS   Behold him.   [*Draws the curtain and discovers Pericles.*]
                    This was a goodly person
Till the disaster that, one mortal night,
Drove him to this.   35

LYSIMACHUS   Sir King, all hail! The gods preserve you!
Hail, royal sir!

---

12. **aught:** all. 18. **whence you are:** where you come from. 24-25. **nor taken sustenance/ But to prorogue his grief:** eat no more than will sustain grief. 26. **distemperature:** despair. 27. **'Twould:** It would. 31. **bootless:** useless. 35. **Drove him to this:** self-neglect. Recall that Pericles has refused to wash or shave for some time.

HELICANUS	It is in vain; he will not speak to you.†

HELICANUS   It is in vain; he will not speak to you.†

LORD   Sir, we have a maid in Mytilene; I durst wager
Would win some words of him.

LYSIMACHUS   'Tis well bethought. 40
She, questionless, with her sweet harmony
And other chosen attractions, would allure,
And make a batt'ry through his deafen'd parts,
Which now are midway stopp'd.
She is all happy as the fairest of all, 45
And, with her fellow maids, is now upon
The leafy shelter that abuts against
The island's side.   [*Gives an order to a Lord, who exit.*]

HELICANUS   Sure, all effectless! yet nothing we'll omit
That bears recovery's name. But since your kindness 50
We have stretch'd thus far, let us beseech you
That for our gold we may provision have,
Wherein we are not destitute for want,
But weary for the staleness.

LYSIMACHUS   O, sir, a courtesy
Which if we should deny, the most just gods 55
For every graff would send a caterpillar,
And so inflict our province. Yet once more
Let me entreat to know at large the cause
Of your king's sorrow.

HELICANUS   Sit, sir; I will recount it to you.
But see, I am prevented.

    Enter [Lord, with] Marina [and a young Lady].

LYSIMACHUS   O, here is 60
The lady that I sent for. Welcome, fair one!
Is't not a goodly presence?

HELICANUS   She's a gallant lady.

---

42. **Would win some words of him:** Would get him to talk. —**allure:** entice, suggesting that Marina's physical charms are still being put to good use. In the modern vernacular, she seems to be more geisha than a common prostitute. 43. **parts:** including, presumably, his heart *and* his phallus. The idea seems to be that she will charm and awaken his desire for life. 52. **provision:** supplies. 56. **For every graff would send a caterpillar:** Roughly, every new vine grown is eaten by caterpillars. A plague or curse of the gods. 62. **Is't:** Is she not.

---

†   In Neil Bartlett's 2003 Lyric Hammersmith production, Will Keen, dressed in gold pajamas, played a "grieving Howard Hughes, with uncut hair and unending silences" (Benedict Nightingale, "Pericles: the comeback." *The Times*, September 20, 2003).

LYSIMACHUS	She's such a one that, were I well assur'd
	Came of a gentle kind and noble stock,
	I'd wish no better choice, and think me rarely wed. 65
	Fair one, all goodness that consists in bounty
	Expect even here, where is a kingly patient.
	If that thy prosperous and artificial feat
	Can draw him but to answer thee in aught,
	Thy sacred physic shall receive such pay 70
	As thy desires can wish.
MARINA	Sir, I will use
	My utmost skill in his recovery,
	Provided that none but I and my companion maid
	Be suffered to come near him.
LYSIMACHUS	Come, let us leave her;
	And the gods make her prosperous! 75
	[*Marina sings*]‡
LYSIMACHUS	Mark'd he your music?
MARINA	No, nor look'd on us.
LYSIMACHUS	See, she will speak to him.
MARINA	Hail, sir! my lord, lend ear.
PERICLES	Hum, ha! [*Pushes her away.*]
MARINA	I am a maid, 80
	My lord, that ne'er before invited eyes,
	But have been gaz'd on like a comet. She speaks,
	My lord, that, may be, hath endur'd a grief
	Might equal yours, if both were justly weigh'd.
	Though wayward fortune did malign my state, 85
	My derivation was from ancestors

63-64. **I well assur'd/ Came of a gentle kind and noble stock:** She is open to discussing her parentage with Pericles openly at 5.1.85-87 and 5.1.114-115, yet at 5.1.182-184 we hear of her reticence to do so with others. 70. **sacred physic:** Suggesting, perhaps, of some sort of bewitching spell, enchantment. Note that Marina sings to him, just as Cerimon played music to Thaisa. The music of the spheres, 5.1.223, further highlights the connection between music and healing. 72. **utmost:** full. 73. **companion maid:** The companion has no lines and serves no purpose. Perhaps the actor offered musical accompaniment? 78. **lend ear:** listen. 81. **invited eyes:** invited men to look at me. 85. **wayward:** See 4.4.10. 86. **derivation:** birth, family line.

---

‡   No song is found in any of the early versions of *Pericles*. The BBC (dir. David Jones, 1984) added a new lyric by Martin Best. John Retallack's Oxford Stage Company created a song that echoed aspects of Antiochus' incest riddle (Paul Taylor, "Make no mistake." *The Independent*, August 17, 1993).

	Who stood equivalent with mighty kings;	
	But time hath rooted out my parentage,	
	And to the world and awkward casualties	
	Bound me in servitude. [*Aside.*] I will desist;	90
	But there is something glows upon my cheek,	
	And whispers in mine ear "Go not till he speak."	

PERICLES   My fortunes—parentage—good parentage—
              To equal mine—Was it not thus? What say you?

MARINA   I said, my lord, if you did know my parentage,   95
              You would not do me violence.

PERICLES   I do think so. Pray you turn your eyes upon me.
              You are like something that—What countrywoman?
              Here of these shores?

MARINA   No, nor of any shores.
              Yet I was mortally brought forth, and am   100
              No other than I appear.

PERICLES   I am great with woe, and shall deliver weeping.
              My dearest wife was like this maid, and such a one*
              My daughter might have been. My queen's square brows;
              Her stature to an inch; as wand-like straight;   105
              As silver-voic'd; her eyes as jewel-like,
              And cas'd as richly; in pace another Juno;
              Who starves the ears she feeds, and makes them hungry,
              The more she gives them speech. Where do you live?

MARINA   Where I am but a stranger. From the deck   110
              You may discern the place.

PERICLES   Where were you bred?

---

89. **awkward:** unlucky, crooked, painful. 96. **You would not do me violence:** Suggesting that Pericles pushed her away; note line 5.1.79. 99. **nor of any shores:** She was born at sea, thus of no shore. 102. **deliver weeping:** pregnant, full of tears. 103. **My dearest wife was like this maid:** The likeness suggests that the same boy actor who played Thaisa doubled here as Marina. Note that an older Thaisa, who reappears in 5.3., looks nothing like her younger self—Pericles clearly does not recognize her. See 5.3.15-20. Another boy actor probably played the older Thaisa. Thus, Pericles here looks into the face of his child and sees the same actor who, earlier, played his wife. See HOW TO READ *PERICLES, PRINCE OF TYRE* AS PERFORMANCE. 110-111. **deck…place:** The sea, seen from the deck of the ship.

*   John Dryden argued that it made little sense for Pericles to escape Antiochus' court in Act 1, only to run the risk of repeating his crime in Act 5. See also the Oxford editor Roger Warren, who believes that Pericles' own incestuous desire was "a danger narrowly averted" (233). On the other hand, Arden editor F.D. Hoeniger disagrees, calling Pericles "a man without defect" (LXXXI); the Cambridge editors Doreen DelVecchio and Anthony Hammond dismiss all talk of incest here as a "doggedly post-modern misreading" (22.n.1). For more on this issue and on how doubling may have underscored the similarities between Marina and Thaisa, see 2.2.8, above, and HOW TO READ *PERICLES, PRINCE OF TYRE* AS PERFORMANCE.

	And how achiev'd you these endowments which	
	You make more rich to owe?	
MARINA	If I should tell my history, it would seem	
	Like lies disdain'd in the reporting.	

PERICLES   Prithee speak!   115
Falseness cannot come from thee; for thou lookest
Modest as Justice, and thou seem'st a palace
For the crown'd truth to dwell in. I will believe thee,
And make my senses credit thy relation
To points that seem impossible; for thou lookest   120
Like one I lov'd indeed. What were thy friends?
Didst thou not say, when I did push thee back
(Which was when I perceiv'd thee) that thou cam'st
From good descending?

MARINA   So indeed I did.

PERICLES Report thy parentage. I think thou said'st   125
Thou hadst been toss'd from wrong to injury,
And that thou thought'st thy griefs might equal mine,
If both were opened.

MARINA   Some such thing
I said, and said no more but what my thoughts
Did warrant me was likely.

PERICLES   Tell thy story.   130
If thine considered prove the thousand part
Of my endurance, thou art a man, and I
Have suffered like a girl. Yet thou dost look
Like patience gazing on kings' graves and smiling
Extremity out of act. What were thy friends?   135
How lost thou them? Thy name, my most kind virgin?
Recount, I do beseech thee. Come, sit by me.

MARINA My name is Marina.

PERICLES   O, I am mock'd,
And thou by some incensed god sent hither
To make the world to laugh at me.

---

113. **You make more rich to owe:** gifts/skills, made more rich in possessing/mastering. 115. **Like lies disdain'd in the reporting:** Roughly, no one believes my story. 119. **credit thy relation:** believe your story. 120-121. **lookest/ Like one I lov'd indeed:** See 5.1.103, above. 126. **toss'd:** as on the sea. 128. **opened:** examined, compared, discussed. 129-130. **what my thoughts/Did warrant me was likely:** Roughly, what I felt to be true intuitively. 134. **Like patience gazing on kings' graves and smiling:** A common figure in graveyards, possibly inspired by images of the Roman goddess Patientia. 139. **incensed:** angry, vengeful.

MARINA	Patience, good sir,	140
	Or here I'll cease.	
PERICLES	Nay, I'll be patient.	

MARINA   Patience, good sir,   140
Or here I'll cease.

PERICLES   Nay, I'll be patient.
Thou little know'st how thou dost startle me
To call thyself Marina.

MARINA   The name was given me by one that had some power—
My father, and a king.

PERICLES   How? a king's daughter?   145
And call'd Marina?

MARINA   You said you would believe me;
But, not to be a troubler of your peace,
I will end here.

PERICLES   But are you flesh and blood?
Have you a working pulse? and are no fairy?
No motion? Well, speak on. Where were you born?   150
And wherefore call'd Marina?

MARINA   Call'd Marina
For I was born at sea.

PERICLES   At sea? What mother?

MARINA   My mother was the daughter of a king;
Who died the very minute I was born,
As my good nurse Lychorida hath oft   155
Delivered weeping.

PERICLES   O, stop there a little!
[*Aside.*] This is the rarest dream that e'er dull sleep
Did mock sad fools with. This cannot be.
My daughter's buried.—Well, where were you bred?
I'll hear you more, to th' bottom of your story,   160
And never interrupt you.

MARINA   You'll scarce believe me;
'Twere best I did give o'er.

PERICLES   I will believe you by the syllable
Of what you shall deliver. Yet give me leave:
How came you in these parts? Where were you bred?   165

MARINA   The King my father did in Tharsus leave me,
Till cruel Cleon, with his wicked wife,

---

141. **patient:** calm. 149. **fairy:** a changling, assuming a mortal form. 156. **Delivered weeping:** Told while weeping, playing on delivery, birth. 160. **th' bottom of your story:** to the end of your history. 162. **give o'er:** remain silent. 164. **me leave:** permission to ask.

Did seek to murther me; and having woo'd
A villain to attempt it, who having drawn to do't,
A crew of pirates came and rescued me;   170
Brought me to Mytilene. But, good sir,
Whither will you have me? Why do you weep? It may be,
You think me an imposture. No, good faith!
I am the daughter to King Pericles,
If good King Pericles be.

PERICLES   Ho, Helicanus!   175

HELICANUS   Calls my lord?

PERICLES   Thou art a grave and noble counsellor,
Most wise in general. Tell me, if thou canst,
What this maid is, or what is like to be,
That thus hath made me weep?

HELICANUS   I know not; but   180
Here is the regent, sir, of Mytilene
Speaks nobly of her.

LYSIMACHUS   She would never tell
Her parentage. Being demanded that,
She would sit still and weep.

PERICLES   O Helicanus, strike me, honor'd sir,   185
Give me a gash, put me to present pain,
Lest this great sea of joys rushing upon me
O'erbear the shores of my mortality
And drown me with their sweetness. O, come hither,
Thou that beget'st him that did thee beget;   190
Thou that wast born at sea, buried at Tharsus,
And found at sea again! O Helicanus,
Down on thy knees, thank the holy gods as loud
As thunder threatens us. This is Marina.
What was thy mother's name? Tell me but that,   195
For truth can never be confirm'd enough,
Though doubts did ever sleep.

MARINA   First, sir, I pray,
What is your title?

---

168. **murther:** murder. 172. **Whither will you have me:** Roughly, where would you lead me? 179. **what is like to be:** What has just passed. 186-189. **Give me a gash…sweetness:** Roughly, pinch me or I'll die of joy. 190. **Thou that beget'st him that did thee beget:** Roughly, you have renewed me, made me young again, though there is a hint of incest here, echoing 1.1.128. 194. **As thunder threatens us:** Roughly, it would be impious not to thank the gods for this miracle. 197. **Though doubts did ever sleep:** Roughly, though all my doubts are already at rest.

PERICLES	I am Pericles of Tyre. But tell me now
	My drown'd queen's name, as in the rest you said 200
	Thou hast been godlike perfect.
	The heir of kingdoms, and another life
	To Pericles thy father.
MARINA	Is it no more to be your daughter than
	To say my mother's name was Thaisa? 205
	Thaisa was my mother, who did end
	The minute I began.
PERICLES	Now blessing on thee! Rise; thou art my child.
	Give me fresh garments. Mine own, Helicanus!
	She is not dead at Tharsus, as she should have been, 210
	By savage Cleon. She shall tell thee all;
	When thou shalt kneel, and justify in knowledge
	She is thy very princess.—Who is this?
HELICANUS	Sir, 'tis the Governor of Mytilene,
	Who, hearing of your melancholy state, 215
	Did come to see you.
PERICLES	I embrace you.
	Give me my robes. I am wild in my beholding.
	O heavens bless my girl! [*Music.*] But hark, what music?
	Tell Helicanus, my Marina, tell him
	O'er, point by point, for yet he seems to doubt, 220
	How sure you are my daughter. But what music?
HELICANUS	My lord, I hear none.
PERICLES	None?
	The music of the spheres! List, my Marina.
LYSIMACHUS	It is not good to cross him. Give him way.
PERICLES	Rarest sounds! Do ye not hear? 225
LYSIMACHUS	Music, my lord? I hear.
PERICLES	Most heavenly music!
	It nips me unto list'ning, and thick slumber
	Hangs upon mine eyes. Let me rest. [*Sleeps.*]

---

202. **another life:** Roughly, make me feel alive again, give me reason to live. 206. **end:** died. 210. **as she should have been:** Roughly, as we believed. 211. **By savage Cleon:** Cleon's sole guilt is open to debate. See Epilogue 11-12. 212. **justify in knowledge:** judge by this new revelation, knowledge. 217. **I am wild in my beholding:** giddy with happiness. 223. **The music of the spheres:** Music generated by the heavens moving in accord. That Pericles hears it suggests that his destiny is now in alignment with the heavens—his bad luck and troubles are over. —**List:** Listen. 224. **cross:** interrupt, distract. 227. **nips:** tastes, entices.

LYSIMACHUS	A pillow for his head! So, leave him all.
	Well, my companion friends, if this but answer 230
	To my just belief, I'll well remember you.[*Exeunt all but Pericles.*]

Diana [appears].

DIANA	My temple stands in Ephesus. Hie thee thither
	And do upon mine altar sacrifice.
	There, when my maiden priests are met together,
	Before the people all 235
	Reveal how thou at sea didst lose thy wife.
	To mourn thy crosses, with thy daughter's, call,
	And give them repetition to the life.
	Or perform my bidding, or thou livest in woe;
	Do it, and happy—by my silver bow! 240
	Awake, and tell thy dream. [*Vanishes.*]
PERICLES	Celestial Dian, goddess argentine,
	I will obey thee. Helicanus!

[Enter Helicanus, Lysimachus, and Marina.]

HELICANUS	Sir?
PERICLES	My purpose was for Tharsus, there to strike
	The inhospitable Cleon; but I am 245
	For other service first. Toward Ephesus
	Turn our blown sails; eftsoons I'll tell thee why.
	[*To Lysimachus*] Shall we refresh us, sir, upon your shore,
	And give you gold for such provision
	As our intents will need? 250
LYSIMACHUS	Sir, with all my heart; and, when you come ashore,
	I have another suit.
PERICLES	You shall prevail,
	Were it to woo my daughter; for it seems
	You have been noble towards her.
LYSIMACHUS	Sir, lend me your arm.
PERICLES	Come, my Marina. *Exeunt.* 255

---

231. **To my just belief, I'll well remember you:** Difficult. Perhaps in reference to Marina. Roughly, if she really is, as I believe her now to be, a princess, I'll reward you all. 232. **Hie thee hither:** travel there. 237. **crosses:** bad luck. 242. **argentine:** from *argentinus*, silvery, like the moon. See 5.3.7 below. 245. **inhospitable Cleon:** Pericles blames Cleon more than Dionyza. See also Epilogue 11-12. 247. **eftsoons:** soon. 250. **intents:** plans, future voyages. 252. **I have another suit:** Roughly, I have a favor to ask. He wants to marry Pericles' daughter. 254. **noble:** good, decent.

SCENE II. [*Before the Temple of Diana at Ephesus.*]

Enter Gower.

GOWER   Now our sands are almost run;
                More a little, and then dumb.
                This, my last boon, give me,
                For such kindness must relieve me:
                That you aptly will suppose   5
                What pageantry, what feats, what shows,
                What minstrelsy and pretty din
                The regent made in Mytilin
                To greet the King. So he thrived
                That he is promis'd to be wived   10
                To fair Marina; but in no wise
                Till he had done his sacrifice,
                As Dian bade; whereto being bound,
                The interim, pray you, all confound.
                In feather'd briefness sails are fill'd,   15
                And wishes fall out as they're will'd.
                At Ephesus the temple see,
                Our king, and all his company.
                That he can hither come so soon
                Is by your fancies' thankful doom.   *Exit.* 20

SCENE III. [*The Temple of Diana*† *at Ephesus; Thaisa standing near the altar, as High Priestess; a number of Virgins on each side; Cerimon and other Ephesians attending.*]

Enter Pericles, Lysimachus, Helicanus, Marina, and others.

PERICLES   Hail, Dian! To perform thy just command,
              I here confess myself the King of Tyre;

SCENE II.
1. **sands:** sands of time. 2. **dumb:** silence. 3. **boon:** favor. 7. **din:** noise, celebration. 8. **regent:** Lysimachus. 12. **his sacrifice:** Not Lysimachus' sacrifice, but Pericles'. 13-14. **being bound...all confound:** No marriage can take place until Pericles completes his voyage to the temple of Diana. 15. **feather'd briefness:** Quick as birds in flight. 20. **doom:** judgment, decision—ie. in your imaginative power.

---

†   In a joint Royal Shakespeare Company and Cardboard Citizens production (dir. Adrian Jackson, 2003), Diana's Temple was "a kitsch shrine to Princess Di complete with a huge publicity shot and a statuette of her as the Madonna" (Kate Bassett, "All washed up (on a shore of wet jumpers)." *Independent on Sunday,* August 3, 2003).

Who, frighted from my country, did wed
At Pentapolis the fair Thaisa.
At sea in childbed died she, but brought forth   5
A maid child call'd Marina; who, O goddess,
Wears yet thy silver livery. She at Tharsus
Was nurs'd with Cleon; who at fourteen years
He sought to murder; but her better stars
Brought her to Mytilene; 'gainst whose shore   10
Riding, her fortunes brought the maid aboard us,
Where, by her own most clear remembrance, she
Made known herself my daughter.

THAISA   Voice and favor!
You are, you are—O royal Pericles!   [*Swoons.*]

PERICLES   What means the nun? She dies! Help, gentlemen!   15

CERIMON   Noble sir,
If you have told Diana's altar true,
This is your wife.

PERICLES   Reverent appearer, no.
I threw her overboard with these very arms.

CERIMON   Upon this coast, I warrant you.

PERICLES   'Tis most certain.   20

CERIMON   Look to the lady. O, she's but over-joy'd.
Early in blustering morn this lady was
Thrown upon this shore. I op'd the coffin,
Found there rich jewels; recovered her, and plac'd her
Here in Diana's temple.

PERICLES   May we see them?   25

CERIMON   Great sir, they shall be brought you to my house,
Whither I invite you. Look, Thaisa is
Recovered.

THAISA   O, let me look!
If he be none of mine, my sanctity
Will to my sense bend no licentious ear,   30

SCENE III.
3. **frighted:** scared off. As detailed in 1.2.117-18. 5. **maid child:** female child. 7. **silver livery:** silver, the colour of the moon, sacred to Diana. See 5.1.242. 9. **better:** lucky, guiding. 11. **Riding:** the ship riding/lying in anchor. 17. **If you have:** If what you have told. 21. **over-joy'd:** Not dead, as Pericles thinks. This is the second time that he thinks she's dead. 24. **recovered:** healed. 25. **them:** The contents of the coffin. He seems to need proof. 30. **my sense bend no licentious ear:** Roughly, if he is not my husband, I won't be attracted to him.

Pericles, 1947, directed by Nugent Monck, designed by Barry Jackson. The photograph shows the temple of Diana (Diana Mahoney, central tripod). The other cast, from left to right, includes Lysimachus (Myles Eason, left tripod), Thaisa (Irene Sutcliffe, centre left), Pericles (Paul Scofield, centre), Marina (Daphne Slater, centre right, white dress). (Angus McBean © Royal Shakespeare Company)

	But curb it, spite of seeing. O my lord,	
	Are you not Pericles? Like him you spake;	
	Like him you are. Did you not name a tempest,	
	A birth, and death?	
PERICLES	The voice of dead Thaisa!	
THAISA	That Thaisa am I, supposed dead	35
	And drown'd.	
PERICLES	Immortal Dian!	
THAISA	Now I know you better.	
	When we with tears parted Pentapolis,	
	The King my father gave you such a ring. *[Shows a ring.]*	
PERICLES	This, this! No more, you gods! your present kindness	40
	Makes my past miseries sports. You shall do well	

33. **name:** speak of. 41. **Makes my past miseries sports:** Roughly, this joy turns all my miseries into inconsequential afterthoughts.

	That on the touching of her lips I may	
	Melt and no more be seen. O, come, be buried	
	A second time within these arms!	
MARINA	My heart	
	Leaps to be gone into my mother's bosom. [*Kneels to Thaisa.*]	45
PERICLES	Look who kneels here! Flesh of thy flesh, Thaisa;	
	Thy burden at the sea, and call'd Marina	
	For she was yielded there.	
THAISA	Blest, and mine own!	
HELICANUS	Hail, madam, and my queen!	
THAISA	I know you not.	
PERICLES	You have heard me say, when I did fly from Tyre,	50
	I left behind an ancient substitute.	
	Can you remember what I call'd the man?	
	I have nam'd him oft.	
THAISA	'Twas Helicanus then.	
PERICLES	Still confirmation!	
	Embrace him, dear Thaisa; this is he.	55
	Now do I long to hear how you were found;	
	How possibly preserv'd; and who to thank,	
	Besides the gods, for this great miracle.	
THAISA	Lord Cerimon, my Lord. This is the man,	
	Through whom the gods have shown their power, that can	60
	From first to last resolve you.	
PERICLES	Reverent sir,	
	The gods can have no mortal officer	
	More like a god than you. Will you deliver	
	How this dead queen relives?	
CERIMON	I will, my lord.	
	Beseech you first, go with me to my house,	65
	Where shall be shown you all was found with her;	
	How she came placed here in the temple;	
	No needful thing omitted.	
PERICLES	Pure Dian, bless thee for thy vision! I	
	Will offer night oblations to thee. Thaisa,	70

43-44. **O, come, be buried/A second time within these arms:** Roughly, buried in my arms, we will both be renewed, reborn. 46. **Flesh of thy flesh:** Uneasily echoing the incest of 1.1.131. See also 5.1.103, above. 51. **ancient substitute:** reverend man who acted as my regent. 57. **preserv'd:** saved. 70. **night of oblations:** prayers; at night because of Diana's association with the moon. See 5.3.7.

Pericles, 1989, directed by David Thacker, designed by Fran Thompson. The photograph shows Marina (Suzan Sylvester, left), Pericles (Nigel Terry, centre) and Thaisa (Sally Edwards, right) reunited. (Joe Cocks Studio Collection © Shakespeare Birthplace Trust)

	This prince, the fair betrothed of your daughter,	
	Shall marry her at Pentapolis. And now	
	This ornament	
	Makes me look dismal will I clip to form;	
	And what this fourteen years no razor touch'd,	75
	To grace thy marriage day I'll beautify.	
THAISA	Lord Cerimon hath letters of good credit, sir,	
	My father's dead.	
PERICLES	Heavens make a star of him! Yet there, my queen,	
	We'll celebrate their nuptials, and ourselves	80
	Will in that kingdom spend our following days.	
	Our son and daughter shall in Tyrus reign.	
	Lord Cerimon, we do our longing stay	
	To hear the rest untold. Sir, lead's the way.	*Exeunt.*

73. **This ornament:** his unshaved and filthy beard. 79. **Heavens make a star of him:** Roughly, may his goodness shine forever. In Greek Myth, the Pleiades star cluster was made of nymphs Zeus turned into stars.

EPILOGUE

Enter Gower.

GOWER   In Antiochus and his daughter you have heard
Of monstrous lust the due and just reward;
In Pericles, his queen, and daughter, seen,
Although assail'd with fortune fierce and keen,
Virtue preserv'd from fell destruction's blast,   5
Led on by heaven, and crown'd with joy at last.
In Helicanus may you well descry
A figure of truth, of faith, of loyalty.
In reverend Cerimon there well appears
The worth that learned charity aye wears.   10
For wicked Cleon and his wife, when fame
Had spread their cursed deed, the honor'd name
Of Pericles, to rage the city turn,
That him and his they in his palace burn.
The gods for murder seemed so content   15
To punish them—although not done, but meant.
So, on your patience evermore attending,
New joy wait on you! Here our play has ending.   [*Exit.*]

EPILOGUE
2. **the due and just reward:** Blaming the daughter for her father's violation seems extreme to our twenty-first century temperaments. See note for Prologue 26. 7. **descry:** observe. 10. **aye:** always. 11. **wicked Cleon and his wife:** Surely Dionyza is more to blame than Cleon. Her crime was attempted murder; his involved only the cover-up.

HOW TO READ *PERICLES, PRINCE OF TYRE* AS PERFORMANCE

Shakespeare is not just an author taught in English classes; he is also a cornerstone of Western theater. While many of you may be reading this text as part of an English survey class, it is paramount to bear in mind that *Pericles* and his other plays were meant to be staged, not read. If reading novels or poems present their own problems of intention and nuance, Shakespeare's plays present additional challenges, in that theatrical performance is collaborative, and, thus, the meaning of the play varies from cast to cast and era to era. Yet, if *Pericles* is complete only in the crucible of performance, can we (and should we) say that Shakespeare's plays have no intrinsic meaning? Certainly, the history of Shakespearean performance indicates the plasticity of the scripts. However, the end results, no matter how different, probably stem from a similar set of questions, which are of use to both readers and to performers of the play. In addition to exploring some of these questions, I will also offer my own concrete experiences as dramaturge for a 2002 University of La Verne student production.

Thinking of a Shakespeare play as meant for the stage can be initially disorientating for many English majors. We are taught, principally, to study character, theme, and plot. But imagine that you are a teacher who has been asked to direct the play. For anyone bent on bringing *Pericles* to the stage, a number of additional logistical factors will have to be overcome. Where exactly will you stage *Pericles*, and how will that space affect your presentation? If you have a multi-level set, you might want to have Gower come out on an upper balcony and present the action taking place on the main stage below. On the other hand, while this makes some initial sense, you will be faced with a problem: What will you do with Gower for the rest of the play? If he simply takes a seat on the upper balcony and observes the action, audiences might find themselves drifting from the action of the play to observing Gower's reaction to it. If directing within a proscenium arch theater—think of a big TV box with the action happening within it—audiences may feel removed from the action, and Gower's narrative frame, essentially another layer of separation, may alienate them still more. Staging *Pericles* in a park has its own issues. At least in a modern theater you can dim the lights to suggest the end of a scene or a break of some sort. Entrances and exits in a park or in the round will have to be worked out meticulously. And then there is the shipwreck. A state-of-the art theatre can create nearly as many special effects as found in a *Star Wars* movie, but getting an audience to believe, without the aid of movie magic, that a ship is being tossed about on the high seas, when in reality your actors are standing on a manicured lawn, may prove difficult.

In casting and in costume, choices will have to be made. Will you opt for an all male cast, attempting to recreate the historical dynamic of Shakespeare's original company? On the one hand, this may make sense, if you wanted to create a historically accurate production. On the other hand, an all male production might be seen by many in the audience as a political statement on gay marriage or gay rights. You may not object to that, but it may not have been your point either. Another issue to consider: Will you have one actor playing one part, or will you double-up roles? The play does have a variety of small parts. If you cast an actor to play just Antiochus, you will have him on for the first act, but what is that actor to do for the rest of the play? In a school production, where actors are performing gratis, that may not be an issue. In a professional production, paying someone to do nothing for four acts is economically unsound. And what about costumes? The play is set in the ancient Mediterranean. Do we want Prince Pericles in a Greek toga, or do we want some leeway here? In the nineteenth century, many Shakespeare directors felt it was necessary to create a sense of historical verisimilitude. The rehearsal for Charles Kean's *King Lear* offers a prime example. When, in the action of the play, one actor gave another a key, Kean interrupted: "Good heavens!" he shouted to the actor playing Edmund, "you give it …as if it was a common room-door key. Let the audience see it, sir; make 'em feel it; impress upon 'em that it is a *key of the period*, sir."[1] On the other hand, creating a museum-piece setting can make audiences feel that the play is not speaking to their own issues. Using mixed costume, particularly modern costume, may allow some audience members to feel that, despite the archaic language, the play has a trans-historical nature—that it can still speak to their concerns. In the brothel scenes, for example, you might have the prostitutes in punk gear, or have some of them shooting or snorting drugs— simple actions by which the director may comment on inner-city economic blight, adolescent ennui, drug use, or the spread of AIDs and other sexual diseases.

Then there is the issue of Shakespeare's language. *Pericles* offers quite a bit of prose, but the major, aristocratic figures, particularly Pericles himself, speak almost entirely in verse. Do you want Pericles' language to retain its high poetic formulation, or will you suggest to your lead actor that he deliver his poetic lines as if he were merely speaking prose? You are dealing here with the issue not only of language but also of its forms. Reading poetry as prose may impoverish the lines; however, keep in mind that in the hands of a weak actor, your poetic Pericles may come across as overly dramatic or just plain silly.

---

1   Charles E.L. Wingate, *Shakespeare's Heroes on the Stage* (New York: Thomas Y. Crowell & Company, 1896), 93.

Perhaps you don't have enough actors or time to stage a full version. It may seem like sacrilege to some, but there is nothing wrong with cutting characters or whole scenes or rearranging their order. Many scholars now believe that Shakespeare wrote a maximal script—a script larger than it needed to be—in part to give his company some useful choices. In essence, Shakespeare seems to have written his plays as textual play-doh, ready to be shaped in any number of ways: a full production might be shaped for the Globe, another shorter version might be moulded for a smaller touring cast, etc. Perhaps you'd like to cut out Act 1, or the character of Gower?

No matter the amount of play-text involved, you will need some sort of shape or internal coherence, what a director might call an interpretation or through-line. This can be a tricky thing. If, on the one hand, you use the play to make a comment on, say, the war in Iraq, you may be accused of taking liberties with the text. On the other hand, Pericles is a refugee, fleeing from war or the threat of it. The art of interpretation is to pick a theme—and a way of expressing that theme—that fits the play. Your interpretation is your own, but it should, at least in part, open the audience to the brilliance of the text, rather than the passion of your politics.

Theatre can be liberating, a place for free-thinking, but it can also be a resource for scholarly exploration. For example, in my work as dramaturge on the play, I was struck by the opening issue of incest and Pericles' later exchange with Marina. I spent many weeks and months wondering whether scholars were correct in thinking that Shakespeare abandoned Wilkins' first two acts in favor of a three act play (Acts 3-5) that made little or no attempt to link up with what had come before. Perhaps Shakespeare did write only Acts 3-5, but the idea that the overriding theme of incest at the beginning of the play was utterly abandoned seemed somehow wrong.[2] There was, to my mind, a circularity to Pericles' encounter with his daughter, one that concluded the issue of Antiochus and his offspring.

A little bit of digging revealed that I was not alone in this thought. The Restoration playwright and poet John Dryden wrote: "Pericles, Prince of Tyre, must not be in danger in the fifth act, of committing incest with his daughter."[3] Further, this was an old worry that just wouldn't go away: In 1987, Ruth Nevo argued that Pericles was haunted by the fear of incest; in 1996, Maria Teresa Macaela Prendergast argued that the play contains three incestuous pairings: Antiochus and his daughter, Cleon and his daughter, and Pericles and Marina; in 2001, Stephen Orgel argued that the "incest plot resonates throughout the play."[4]

In my early discussions with the director, Georgij Paro, I presented this information, and we agreed to explore whether the idea of Pericles having some incestuous desire for his daughter might work in performance. Encouraged by our

---

2   For more on Wilkins' possible role in writing *Pericles*, see Introduction.

3   John Dryden, *Essays of John Dryden* (London and New York: Macmillan and Co, 1985), 159.

4   Ruth Nevo, *Shakespeare's Other Language* (New York and London: Methuen and Co, 1987), 42; Maria Teresa Macaela Prendergast "Engendering *Pericles.*" *Literature and Psychology* XXXXII.4 (1996): 53-75; Stephen Orgel, The Pelican Shakespeare ed. 2001: XLI. See also performance note for 5.1.103.

discussion, I dug further. Unlike Shaw, Shakespeare left no detailed notes to tell his actors what to think and feel in their roles. Figuring out what Pericles was "feeling" when he first saw Marina would be based solely on guess-work. Still, Shakespeare based his play on Gower's and Twine's versions. Might further evidence of Shakespeare's intentions be found in those source materials? In John Gower's original version, Antiochus is blamed fully and solely for his incestuous relationship with his daughter, who is horrified by his overture:

> And she was tender, and full of drede,
> She couth nought hir maydenhede
> Defende (*Confessio Amantis*, BK VIII: 309-312).[5]

In Laurence Twine's version, Antiochus, mourning his lost wife, rapes his daughter, who was so outraged by the act that she tells her nurse that she will commit suicide: "the name of Father is lost in me, so that I can have no remedie now but death onely" (Twine, *The Patterne of Painefull Adventures*, 427).

Shakespeare's version is radically different. His Gower blames both Antiochus *and* his daughter for their incestuous relations:

> the father liking took
> And her to incest did provoke.
> Bad child; worse father! (1.0.25-27)

I wondered, why did Shakespeare make Antiochus' daughter complicit in the incestuous act and what, if any, bearing did that decision have on the fifth act, wherein Pericles is reunited with his daughter?

I was also investigating another problem: a series of missing songs. In 2.5, we have reference to Pericles having sung to his future bride Thaisa:

> *Simonides*: I am beholding to you
> For your sweet music this last night. I do
> Protest my ears were never better fed
> With such delightful pleasing harmony. (2.5.24-27)

The music scene is missing from the extant text, yet many of its details can be found in the Gower source, in which Pericles, therein named Apollonius, takes up a harp and entertains the princess of Pentapolis, his future bride. Moreover, Apollonius takes up the instrument only *after* the princess plays a song on that same instrument. So this missing or cut scene in *Pericles* actually refers to a night of at least *two* songs in which Pericles and his future bride express harmoniously their love for each other. A third, lost song occurs in 5.1, when Marina sings to her father. I wondered, could we be dealing with the same song in all three instances? If Marina wooed Pericles with the same song he sang to his bride and she sang to him, we would have a nice

---

5   All references in this short essay to John Gower's *Confessio Amantis*, Laurence Twine, *The Patterne of Painefull Adventures*, and George Wilkins, *The Painfull Adventures of Pericles Prince of Tyre* are derived from Geoffrey Bullough, *Narrative and Dramatic Sources of Shakespeare*. 8 vols. (London: Routledge and Kegan Paul; New York, Columbia University Press, 1957-75), Vol.VI.

way to link a cast doubling (Marina and Thaisa— more on this anon) with a thematic association (Pericles repeating the terrible sin of Antiochus).

Of course, we would still have to write the song ourselves. In discussions with the director, we agreed that the new song should have the same internal rhythms as Antiochus' poetic riddle. There was sound textual evidence for this. In Twine's version, Marina's song is a riddle of sorts, one in which the Pericles-character must learn the secret of her identity:

> Amongst the harlots foule I walke,
>   yet harlot none I am....
> (Twine, *The Patterne of Painefull Adventures*, 464)

The line is faintly echoed in the verse Antiochus' daughter presents to Pericles:

> I am no viper, yet I feed
> On mother's flesh which did me breed. (1.1.64-65)

To further connect Acts 1-2 to Acts 3-5, we began to experiment with a doubling of Thaisa and Marina. We did so on the premise that Shakespeare had come upon the idea while reading his sources. In Gower, Simonides' daughter has no name, but, soon after she marries the prince, she gives birth to a child, named Thaise. In Twine's version, the daughter is named Tharsia. Shakespeare takes the source name of Pericles' daughter and gives it to Pericles' wife. This confusion of identities, the daughter's name given to the wife, is echoed in the play as well. In Act 5, Pericles sees Marina for the first time and remarks: "My dearest wife was like this maid" (5.1.103). The likeness suggests that the same boy actor who played Thaisa doubled here as Marina. Note that an older Thaisa, who reappears in 5.3, looks nothing like her younger self—Pericles clearly does not recognize her at 5.3.15-20. The inference is that one boy actor played Thaisa in Act 2 and 3 and then played Marina for the rest of the play. Another boy actor played the older Thaisa in 5.3. Thus, when Pericles looks into the face of his child, he sees the same boy actor who, earlier, played his wife. Further, since Antiochus' daughter appears for only one scene, we can assume that this boy actor also played other parts. It is, therefore, entirely possible that a boy actor played Antiochus' daughter and, thereafter, the young Thaisa, and then the equally young Marina. If so, Pericles has run from incest, but, visually speaking, it has followed him, as Dryden suspected, throughout his journey.[6]

In the process of rehearsal, discussion and research, *Pericles*, a play once thought flawed and scattered, was coming together, or, more accurately, was coming full circle thematically. Our hero had not merely to flee Antiochus' court but had also to retrace his nemesis' descent into self pity and, ultimately, into the pit of sin. His triumph over Antiochus came at the last and most perilous moment—when Pericles faced Antiochus' temptation, the temptation to trade solipsistic sorrow for self-absorbing pleasure. By exploring the source materials, we had hit on a darkly biblical story. Like Antiochus, Pericles had lost a wife, and, like Antiochus, he could cheat death— have

---

6   For more on doubling possibilities, see performance note 2.2.8.

his wife again— by embracing a maiden who looks just like her mother. Our Pericles prevailed over temptation, but only by recognizing the vision of consolation presented so temptingly before him. Indeed, Pericles' choice would have been fairly meaningless were he unable to recognize within himself the dark allure of the alternative. As we now saw it, Pericles' story was not that of a hero who redeemed his world, nor was it the story of a man who was redeemed by his world; it was the story of a man who came to recognize that restraint did not extinguish sin in the world or within himself.

But how to express the prince's sinful nature? Should Pericles articulate any desire for his daughter? Shakespeare leaves us only a hint: Marina's reply, "my lord, if you did know my parentage,/ You would not do me violence" (5.1.95-96). Just how violent should our Pericles be, and should that violence be expressed libidinously? Again, the sources were of use here. In Twine's version, the Pericles-character, just before acknowledging his daughter, is overcome by a sudden frenzy:

> Then [Pericles] fell in a rage, and forgetting all courtesie, his
> unbridled affection stirring him thereunto, rose up sodainly, and
> stroke the maiden on the face with his foot, so that shee fell to the
> ground, and the bloud gushed plentifully out of her cheekes.
>
> (466-467)

Confirmation of Pericles' violence was also found in Wilkins' version, wherein Marina chastises Pericles; thereafter, an unexpectedly heated Pericles in "rash distemperature, strucke her on the face"(543). We tried Twine's action in rehearsal, wherein it soon became clear that we were dealing with the distorted signs of rape: affection expressed as violence, the penis violating the hymen, in Twine poetically converted to the foot violently rending his daughter's blood-filled cheek.

Yes, it all made perfect sense, but would it work in the theater? We discussed the idea with various cast members, who, for the most part, remained hostile to the interpretation. Doubling or tripling Antiochus' daughter with Marina and Thaisa naturally infuriated the women in the cast, who, quite correctly, understood that two of them would no longer have speaking roles. In the interests of cast harmony, we scrapped the idea of doubling or tripling these female roles, though we did retain a few doublings. Theater major Samantha Kern, one of our best comic actresses, displayed her talents by performing two characters: one of the fishermen and the broadly comic bawd who runs the whorehouse; Eric Mulholland played another of the fishermen, as well as Gower. Satisfying cast concerns did not end there. Our Pericles, David Rojas, was unhappy with the idea that he had to attack his Marina. As he noted, we were not presenting Gower's or Twine's *Pericles*, but Shakespeare's *Pericles*, and Shakespeare makes it abundantly clear that Pericles does not strike (or poetically violate) Marina but pushes her away. Doesn't this shove suggest that Pericles, rather than attacking or raping Marina, actually fends her off? And does not this indicate that Pericles, rather than wanting to touch his daughter indecorously, doesn't want to touch or be touched by *anybody*? Rojas' objections opened a fruitful discussion, which, oddly, led us back to a more nuanced idea concerning incest. If Pericles had to fend off his daughter, then she, like Antiochus' daughter, was complicit, rather than passive, in an aggressive—though not necessarily sexual—act between father and daughter. Although Marina was not trying to seduce Pericles, her attempt to touch him marked her first willing physical contact with a man since being sold into the Mytilene brothel.

There was another problem. Eric Mulholland, the actor playing Gower, pointed out that such an interpretation—a Pericles plagued by incestuous desire—would be at odds with Gower's line that everyone in the play met their "due and just reward" (Epilogue, 2).[7] Of course, we all agreed that Gower's pronouncement had its own difficulties. Although minor characters such as Cleon, Dionyza, and Antiochus met horrible ends, Pericles was not necessarily recompensed for his patience, nor was he punished for his virtue. While there did seem to be a purpose in the force that wafted Pericles to Antioch, Tyre, Tarsus, Pentapolis, Ephesus, and Mytilene, its meaning, however forceful, remained dark and unfathomable.[8] Still, we had to make a choice here. Just how far were we willing to trust Gower?

Other cast members smoothed over the problem. Pericles had incestuous desire but was not an Antiochus-like villain. We began to think of Pericles as an Oedipus-like figure. After all, Oedipus did not know that the man he had killed was his father or the women that he had married was his mother; similarly, Pericles did not know that the woman who awakened him from his mental and physical lethargy was his daughter, and, if he experienced any desire for her, it was immediately tempered when he learned of Marina's true identity. Besides, even if the prince's thoughts were (possibly) as sinful as Oedipus', his actions were not. Oedipus slept with his mother; Pericles did not sleep with his daughter. In comparing Pericles and Oedipus, the cast agreed that Pericles' end seemed to be more a matter of luck than fortitude. Oedipus found out after the fact that he had committed patricide and incest; Pericles learned of his connection to Marina only moments after noting her similarity to his long-dead queen. This may seem like an inconsequential difference but to contemplate, no matter how briefly, an act, is not the same as putting that contemplation into action. Perhaps this too was part of Shakespeare's point, for it is sometimes difficult to recognize Pericles' abrogated transgression, a sin cut short by moral decency, in a world peopled with so many vicious characters: Antiochus, Thaliard, Dionyza, and Leonine. And yet Shakespeare also drew a variety of characters who, throughout, easily resist the allure of sin: the faithful Helicanus; the good King Simonides; the priestly Thaisa; the maternal Lychorida; the medicinally-minded Cerimon; the virtuous and virginal Marina. Might we add to this list Pericles, who suffers but, unlike Antiochus, never succumbs to sin?

Two days before the official opening, we had a full dress rehearsal and invited a free audience for a preview, followed by a question-and-answer session. We were

---

7   F.D. Hoeniger suggests the play is "not unlike the traditional Christian view [concerning]...the sufferings [of] man" (LXXXVII).

8   The inscrutability of the gods have lead many critics, among them Ernest Schanzer to see the play as an indictment of a "divine Providence" that prosecutes "wholly virtuous characters so cruelly." Ernest Schanzer, Signet Classic Shakespeare ed. 1965: XXXVII.

surprised by the heavy resistance to the Antiochus-Pericles link. The audience needed to pity Pericles; casting him as an incestuous monster hardly seemed like the right way to instill sympathy. The director and I could see and concede the point. Pericles is, after all, the hero, and most audiences want to like and, more importantly, to admire him. They certainly don't want to see him as a pervert—someone who would make an admirable son-in-law for Antiochus. So, one day before our premiere, we cut the staged violence between Pericles and his daughter. Old, weak, and broken-hearted, he would now merely push her away, like a patient who no longer wished to be on life-support.

In the end, the production turned out to be quite different from the way I and the director envisioned it, but the lesson to be learned here is that the director and the cast need not worry that ideas may change in the process of rehearsal. Theatre is a collaborative experiment. Sometimes it will turn out well, sometimes it won't. That is the nature of collaboration. Further, collaboration in the theatre is necessary and unavoidable. Whether performed by professionals, students, or rank amateurs, the director needs to keep in mind that an actor is not an automaton. Each actor, even if taking explicit direction, will add something to the production. A director can direct, but he cannot always just preach to the converted; he will have to listen carefully as well. Ideally, the director and cast are investigators, learning all they can about the play and, in so doing, about themselves, both as individuals and as a group. But the finished product does not have to explain everything learned in the experience. As in film-making, some good stuff will be left on the cutting-room floor. Collaboration is the art of compromise and sacrifice. A great part of the success of a production will depend upon the creativity, the personal chemistry, and the flexibility of the director and cast and, just as importantly and unpredictably, the goodwill of the audience.

TIMELINE

1386(?): John Gower writes *Confessio Amantis*, which contains the earliest version of the *Pericles* story.

1554: *Confessio Amantis* republished.

1564: Shakespeare born.

1567(?): Richard Burbage, Shakespeare's chef tragedian, born. The Red Lion Theatre, the first public playhouse in London, opens.

1576: James Burbage, father of Richard, opens The Theater, in Shoreditch. Lawrence Twine publishes *The Patterne of Painefull Adventures*, based on Gower's version.

1582: Shakespeare marries Anne Hathaway.

1583: Anne Hathaway gives birth to Shakespeare's daughter, Susanna.

1585: Anne Hathaway gives birth to twins, son Hamnet and daughter Judith.

1588(?): Shakespeare leaves for London, begins career as actor and playwright for a variety of companies.

1590(?)-1594: Shakespeare writes *The Comedy of Errors, Titus Andronicus, The Taming of the Shrew, Henry VI, 1,2,3, Richard III, Two Gentlemen of Verona, Love's Labor's Lost*, and his major poems, *Venus and Adonis, The Rape of Lucrece*, and *The Sonnets*.

1594: Shakespeare joins with Richard Burbage as shareholders in The Lord Chamberlain's Men.

1594-1596: Shakespeare writes *Midsummer Night's Dream, Romeo and Juliet, Richard II, Merchant of Venice*.

1596: Hamnet dies, age 11. Richard Burbage purchases Blackfriars, converts it into an indoor playhouse.

1597: James Burbage dies.

1597-1599: Shakespeare writes *Henry IV, 1, 2, Henry V, The Merry Wives of Windsor, As You Like It, Much Ado About Nothing, Julius Caesar*.

1599: The Globe, Shakespeare's main playhouse, built.

1600-1608:   Shakespeare writes *Twelfth Night, Hamlet, Troilus and Cressida, All's Well That Ends Well, Measure for Measure, Othello, King Lear, Macbeth, Antony and Cleopatra, Coriolanus, Timon of Athens*. During this period, Shakespeare's father, John, dies (1601), Shakespeare's company is renamed The King's Men (1603), daughter Susanna marries (1607), his mother, Mary, dies (1608), and his company begins performing plays at Blackfriars (1608).

1606:   George Wilkins publishes the pamphlet, *Three Miseries of Barbary*; he may have been the "G.W." who translated *The historie of Iustine*.

1607:   Lawrence Twine's *The Pattern of Painful Adventures* is republished; George Wilkins writes the play *The Miseries of Enforced Marriage*, co-authors the play *The Travels of the Three English Brothers*; co-authors pamphlet *Jests to make you merie*.

1607-1608:   Shakespeare's *Pericles* written, possibly with additions of George Wilkins, who, in 1608, publishes the novel The *Painfull Adventures of Pericles Prince of Tyre*.

1609:   Shakespeare's play *Pericles* published. The Second Quarto edition is published the same year.

1609-1611:   Shakespeare writes *Cymbeline, The Winter's Tale, The Tempest*.

1610:   *Pericles* performed by the Cholmeley players, a group of travelling actors, at Gowthwaite Halle, Nidderdale, in Yorkshire.

1611:   Third Quarto of *Pericles* published.

1612-1614:   Shakespeare collaborated with John Fletcher on *Henry VIII, The Two Noble Kinsmen*, and a lost play, *Cardenio*.

1616:   Judith Shakespeare married Thomas Quiney; Shakespeare dies, buried in Stratford-upon-Avon.

1619:   Forth Quarto of *Pericles* published; *Pericles* performed at Court, "in the King's great chamber" at Whitehall; Richard Burbage dies.

1623:   First Folio of Shakespeare's plays published, *Pericles* is not included. Anne Hathaway, Shakespeare's widow, dies.

1630:   Fifth Quarto of *Pericles* published.

1631:   *Pericles* performed at the Globe.

1632:   Second Folio published; *Pericles* not included.

1635:   Sixth Quarto of *Pericles* published.

1663:   Third Folio published; *Pericles* not included.

1664:   Second issue of the Third Folio published, *Pericles* included.

Topics for Discussion and Further Study

1. Pericles runs from danger more often than facing it. Compare him to a traditional hero of literature or film. Discuss whether you believe he is heroic or virtuous. In what ways do these characteristics differ?

2. In what ways do Antiochus' and Simonides' personal behaviors reflect upon their respective duties as leaders? Can a good man be a bad king? Can a bad man be a good king?

3. Look at the organization of events. Does Marina's misadventure in Mytilene reiterate any aspect of Pericles' ordeal, or are we dealing with unrelated stories that simply link up at the end?

4. There are a variety of events in the play that are narrated by Gower but are not shown. Was this a matter of technical difficulty—i.e. the limitations of the theatre—or did Shakespeare have some reason for passing over one scene in favor of another?

5. Does it matter if Shakespeare wrote the entire play or only Acts 3-5? If so, why?

6. Shakespeare blames Cleon for the actions of his wife. What does this say about the rights of most women in the early seventeenth century?

7. The play seems to mix Christianity with Greek and Roman Myth. Is a purely Christian moral to the story discernible? In short, is Pericles as much Oedipus as he is Job?

8. Helicanus refuses to take power in Tyre; compare him to Cerimon. What is Shakespeare saying about the virtues and rewards of a moderate life?

9. We may wonder why Thaisa never sends word to her husband or father concerning her miraculous recovery. Look up the term "magic realism" and write a paper on the play's defiance of logic.

10. The events in *Pericles* are guided, ostensibly by Gower but, within the confines of the story, by the gods. In your view, are the gods just?

Performance Issues

1. We know that actors in Shakespeare's company sometimes doubled parts. Put together a chart of the doubling possibilities in the play, then look for ways to double characters according to themes. For example, we might double Antiochus with Cleon to suggest their similar natures or double Helicanus with Thaliard to suggest their differing personalities.

2. Pericles seems to be passive, but he also, off stage, bests the knights at a tourney. In what ways could we stage the play to make Pericles less of a complainer and more pro-active?

3. The sea allows Pericles to bounce around the Mediterranean. What if we staged the play, say, in Kansas? Would a modern-day farm boy on a tractor carry the same message as a prince on a royal ship?

4. Taking just those scenes related to Pericles' daughter, create a new short play entitled *Marina*.

5. Shakespeare's company used boy actors for women's parts. What if we were to cast the play that way today? Write a review from the differing viewpoints of, say, a well-known Sunday televangelist and a well-known spokesperson for the gay community. Are many of your comments generated by the play itself or by modern and often clashing cultural values?

6. Take one scene in the play and modernize its language. Perhaps you might turn one of Gower's speeches into a rap song.

7. Lysimachus met Marina in a whorehouse and was, initially, quite happy to pay for the right to violate her. Write a scenario about the state of their marriage twenty years from their wedding day.

8. Aside from Pericles' dream in 5.1 the gods, while often referenced, do not appear. Cut the Gower scenes and stage the play with the gods actively creating storms, stirring seas, or whispering lines into men's ears.

9. Pander, Boult, and Bawd are hard to differentiate on the page. In what ways might we use costume to suggest their differences? Might we make one (or more) of these characters far more wealthy than another? Might ethnicity be useful? Perhaps Boult is French, while Bawd is Russian. Try a variety of accents.

10 Should a high school production of *Pericles* cut out the brothel scenes? Discuss the benefits and pitfalls of these cuts. Might the play survive expurgation by staging it in creative ways? In 1993, for example, the company Wooden Tongues used puppets for some of the characters. What if we cast Pericles as a woman and Marina as a man? Might a comic adaption, *The Adventures of Periclesa and Marvin*, work?

BIBLIOGRAPHY AND FILMOGRAPHY

The following is a selective list of editions, criticism and film to aid the student. The list is by no means exhaustive. The following texts are widely available in university libraries.

Complete Works

George Lyman Kittredge, *The Kittredge-Players Edition of the Complete Works of William Shakespeare.* New York: Grolier, rpt. 1958.

> The basis for this edition's text, Kittredge's complete works remains an important scholarly achievement.

Stanley Wells and Gary Taylor (eds.), *Shakespeare: The Complete Works.* Oxford: Clarendon Press, 1988.

> While a number of complete works are available, the Wells and Taylor edition is the current gold standard. Individual volumes of each play, with a wide range of detailed critical commentaries, are also available.

Individual Editions of *Pericles*, listed chronologically

Edmond Malone and James Boswell (eds.), *The Plays and Poems of William Shakspeare: With the Corrections and Illustrations of Various Commentators.* London: R. C. and J. Rivington, 1821, vol. 21.

Kenneth Deighton (ed.) *Pericles.* The Arden Shakespeare. Gemn. Ed. W. J. Craig. London: Methuen and CO., 1907.

> These editions contain detailed criticism from a variety of eighteenth-century commentators, many of whom set out the editorial cruxes that shape modern editions. The Malone-Boswell volume is no longer in print, but is available through Google Book Search: http://books. google.com/books?id=Z3I0AAAAMAAJ&printsec=titlepage&source= gbs_summary_r&cad=0.

> Deighton's introduction contains remarkably useful and surprisingly negative assessments of the play from Steevens and Johnson. This

edition is also available online: http://books.google.com/books?id=LVE PAAAAQAAJ&dq=Kenneth+Deighton+(ed.)+Pericles.++The&source=g bs_summary_s&cad=0.

F.D. Hoeniger (ed.) *Pericles*. The Arden Edition of the Works of William Shakespeare. Gen Eds. Harold F. Brooks and Harold Jenkins. London: Methuen & Co, Ltd.; Cambridge, Massachusetts. Harvard University Press, 1963.

> A magisterial case for mixed authorship. Hoeniger weighs the evidence for William Rowley, Thomas Heywood, George Wilkins and John Day. The edition is far weaker on the play's performance history.

Philip Edwards (ed.) *Pericles*. The New Penguin Shakespeare. London and New York: Penguin, 1976; rev. 1996.

> A first-rate pocket-sized edition, but, again, one that sacrifices the play's performance history for textual detail.

Doreen DelVecchio and Anthony Hammond (eds.), *Pericles, Prince of Tyre*, New Cambridge Shakespeare. Gen Eds. Brian Gibbons and A.R. Braunmuller. Cambridge: Cambridge Univeristy Press, 1985.

> An edition that stresses the structural and dramatic strength of the play, argues that Shakespeare was *Pericles'* sole author.

Stephen Orgel (ed.) *Pericles*. The Pelican Shakespeare. Gen. Eds. Stephen Orgel and A.R. Braunmuller. New York and London: Penguin, 2000.

> The notes are sometimes a bit arcane, but there is some commentary concerning the play's theatrical effectiveness.

Roger Warren (ed.), *Pericles*. Oxford and New York: Oxford World Classics, 2003.

> Based on the text found in the abovecited Stanley Wells and Gary Taylor (eds.), *Shakespeare: The Complete Works*. Oxford: Clarendon Press, 1988. The play's performance history is at the forefront for much of the Introduction.

Barbara A, Mowat and Paul Werstine (eds.) *Pericles*. The Folger Shakespeare Library. New York: The Folger Library, 2005

> Concise and clear notes but very little in the way of source study or performance history.

Source Materials

Geoffrey Bullough, *Narrative and Dramatic Sources of Shakespeare*. 8 vols. (London, Routledge and Kegan Paul; New York, Columbia University Press, 1957-75), Vol. VI.

> Excerpts from Gower's *Confessio Amantis*, Laurence Twine, *The Patterne of Painefull Adventures*, Sidney's *Arcadia* and George Wilkins' *The Painfull Adventures of Pericles Prince of Tyre*.

George Wilkins, *The Miseries of Enforced Marriage*. Ed. Glenn H. Blayney. Oxford:

Oxford University Press/The Malone Society Reprints, 1964.

> A minor play, but one that gives the reader of better sense of Wilkins' limited skills.

Recent Criticism (listed chronologically)

E.K. Chambers, *Shakespeare: A Survey*. London: Sedgwick & Jackson, Ltd., 1925.

> Compares *Pericles* to *Timon of Athens* and argues that *Timon* represents Shakespeare in despair; *Pericles* represents Shakespeare in recovery.

C.L. Barber, " 'Thou that Beget'st Him that Did Thee Beget': Transformation in 'Pericles; and 'The Winter's Tale'." *Shakespeare Survey* 22 (1969): 59-67.

> Looks at the generics of comedy and then argues that *Pericles* and Shakespeare's late plays deal with the avoidance of sexual degradation.

Lorraine Helms, "The Saint in the Brothel: Or, Eloquence Rewarded." *Shakespeare Quarterly* 41.3 (1990): 319-32.

> Argues that Marina is based on Seneca's Prostitute Priestess and further notes that Marina's silence concerning her betrothal to Lysimachus links her to a similarly silent Isabella at the end of *Measure for Measure*.

Alexander Leggatt, "The Shadow of Antioch: Sexuality in *Pericles, Prince of Tyre*." *Parallel Lives: Spanish and English National Drama 1580-1680*. Eds. Louise and Peter Forthergill-Payne. Lewisburg, Pennsylvania: Bucknell University Press, 1991. 167-79.

> Compares *Pericles* to other non-Shakespearean plays dealing with incest, including Ford's *'Tis Pity She's a Whore* and Beaumont and Fletcher's *King and No King*; further argues that Pericles' relationship with Marina is tinged with a fear of sexuality.

Stephen J. Lynch, "The Authority of Gower in Shakespeare's *Pericles*." *Mediaevalia* 16 (1993 for 1990): 361-78.

> Examines the complex use of Gower as a narrative device.

Karen Bamford, *Sexual Violence on the Jacobean Stage*. New York: St. Martin's Press, 2000.

> Pages 33-41 and 55-59 examine representations of rape in *Pericles* and other Jacobean plays.

David Skeele (ed.), *Pericles: Critical Essays*. New York: Garland, 2000.

> An outstanding selection of critical commentary and, more vitally, of performance history between 1854 and 1994.

Barbara A. Mowat, "I tell you what mine Authors saye': *Pericles*, Shakespeare, and *Imitatio*." *Archiv* 240 (2003): 42-59.

> Cites the etymology of *author* and its variants *auctor* and *actor* to explore competing views of literary authority.

Charles Nicholl, *The Lodger Shakespeare*. New York and London: Viking/Penguin, 2007.

>Pages 197-226 attempt to answer why Shakespeare would know, much less write a play with, a lowlife like George Wilkins.

Filmography

Pericles (BBC, 1984). Director David Jones, starring Edward Petherbridge (Gower), Mike Gwilym (Pericles), Juliet Stevenson (Thaisa), Amanda Redman (Marina).

>Part of the BBC *Complete Dramatic Works of William Shakespeare*, this video offers a full text with some slight additions, notably a wonderful sword dance in Simonides' court and new song for Marina in 5.1, the latter composed by Martin Best. The TV format reduces the sweep of the action, and the performance is shot on what is clearly a soundstage—unfortunate, since the production is mainly set in deserts which might have offered some *Laurence of Arabia*-like vistas. Director David Jones prefers close-ups and whispered delivery, but this soap-opera technique does not engage the viewer. The main problem is its lack of interpretative through-line. Jones seems to prefer that the play speak for itself. As a result, the actors recite the lines but say nothing particularly original or insightful. The brothel scenes enliven what is otherwise a rather dull affair.